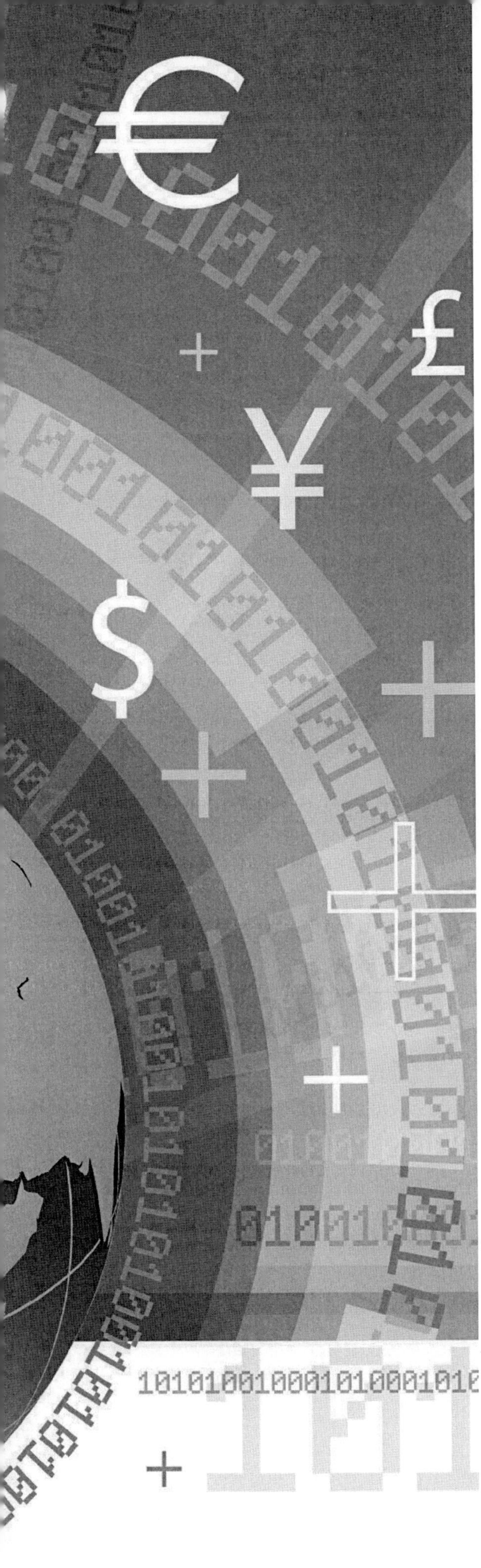

TE FOR
TMENT

Investment Operations Certificate

International Introduction to Securities & Investment

Edition 8, June 2015

This learning manual relates to syllabus version 8.0 and will cover examinations from **10 September 2015 to 9 September 2016**

APPROVED WORKBOOK

Welcome to the Chartered Institute for Securities & Investment's International Introduction to Securities & Investment study material.

This workbook has been written to prepare you for the Chartered Institute for Securities & Investment's International Introduction to Securities & Investment examination.

Published by:
Chartered Institute for Securities & Investment

8 Eastcheap
London
EC3M 1AE
Tel: +44 20 7645 0600
Fax: +44 20 7645 0601

Email: customersupport@cisi.org
www.cisi.org/qualifications

Author:
Kevin Rothwell, Chartered MCSI

Reviewers:
Jonathan Beckett, Chartered MCSI
Julie Harnum, MBA (FS)

This is an educational manual only and the Chartered Institute for Securities & Investment accepts no responsibility for persons undertaking trading or investments in whatever form.

While every effort has been made to ensure its accuracy, no responsibility for loss occasioned to any person acting or refraining from action as a result of any material in this publication can be accepted by the publisher or authors.

A learning map, which contains the full syllabus, appears at the end of this manual. The syllabus can also be viewed on cisi.org and is also available by contacting the Customer Support Centre on +44 20 7645 0777. Please note that the examination is based upon the syllabus. Candidates are reminded to check the Candidate Update area details (cisi.org/candidateupdate) on a regular basis for updates as a result of industry change(s) that could affect their examination.

The questions contained in this manual are designed as an aid to revision of different areas of the syllabus and to help you consolidate your learning chapter by chapter. They should not be seen as a 'mock' examination or necessarily indicative of the level of the questions in the corresponding examination.

Learning manual version: 8.1 (June 2015)

Learning and Professional Development with the CISI

The Chartered Institute for Securities & Investment is the leading professional body for those who work in, or aspire to work in, the investment sector, and we are passionately committed to enhancing knowledge, skills and integrity – the three pillars of professionalism at the heart of our Chartered body.

CISI examinations are used extensively by firms to meet the requirements of government regulators. Besides the regulators in the UK, where the CISI head office is based, CISI examinations are recognised by a wide range of governments and their regulators, from Singapore to Dubai and the US. Around 50,000 examinations are taken each year, and it is compulsory for candidates to use CISI learning manuals to prepare for CISI examinations so that they have the best chance of success. Our learning manuals are normally revised every year by experts who themselves work in the industry and also by our Accredited Training Providers, who offer training and elearning to help prepare candidates for the examinations. Information for candidates is also posted on a special area of our website: cisi.org/candidateupdate.

This learning manual not only provides a thorough preparation for the examination it refers to, it is also a valuable desktop reference for practitioners, and studying from it counts towards your Continuing Professional Development (CPD). Mock examination papers, for most of our titles, will be made available on our website, as an additional revision tool.

CISI examination candidates are automatically registered, without additional charge, as student members for one year (should they not be members of the CISI already), and this enables you to use a vast range of online resources, including CISI TV, free of any additional charge. The CISI has more than 40,000 members, and nearly half of them have already completed relevant qualifications and transferred to a core membership grade. You will find more information about the next steps for this at the end of this manual.

With best wishes for your studies.

Lydia Romero, Director of Learning

It is estimated that this workbook will require approximately 70 hours of study time.

What next?

See the back of this book for details of CISI membership.

Need more support to pass your exam?

See our section on Accredited Training Providers.

Want to leave feedback?

Please email your comments to learningresources@cisi.org

Chapter One

The Financial Services Industry

This syllabus area will provide approximately 2 of the 50 examination questions

1. Introduction

In this chapter, we will look at the role that the financial services industry undertakes within both the local and the global economy.

Stock markets and investment instruments are not unique to one country, and there is increasing similarity in the instruments that are traded on all world markets and in the way that trading and settlement systems are developing.

This chapter looks at how the industry is structured and looks in detail at some of its key participants.

2. The Role of the Financial Services Industry

The world is becoming increasingly integrated and interdependent, as trade and investment flows are global in nature.

With this background, therefore, it is important to understand the core role that the financial services industry performs within the economy and some of the key features of the global financial services sector.

The financial services industry provides the link between organisations needing capital and those with capital available for investment.

For example, an organisation needing capital might be a growing company, and the capital might be provided by individuals saving for their retirement in a pension fund. It is the financial services industry that channels money invested to those organisations that need it, and provides execution, payment, advisory and management services.

It is accepted that the financial services industry plays a critical role in all advanced economies, and that the services it provides can be broken down into three core functions:

- The **investment chain** – through the investment chain, savers and borrowers are brought together. Savers provide financing to businesses, and businesses that wish to grow offer opportunities for savers to take part in the growth and resulting potential returns. The efficiency of this chain is critical to allocating what would otherwise be uninvested capital to businesses that can use it to grow their enterprises, as well as the savings pools of the investors. This chain therefore raises productivity and, in turn, improves the competitiveness of those financial markets within the global economy.
- **Risk** – in addition to the opportunities that the investment chain provides for pooling investment risks, the financial services sector allows other risks to be managed effectively and efficiently through the use of insurance, and increasingly through the use of sophisticated derivatives. These tools help businesses cope with global uncertainties as diverse as the changing value of currencies, the incidence of major accidents or extreme weather conditions. They also help households protect themselves against everyday contingencies.
- **Payment systems** – payment and banking services operated by the financial services sector provide the practical mechanisms for money to be managed, transmitted and received quickly and reliably. It is an essential requirement for commercial activities to take place and for participation in international trade and investment. Access to payment systems and banking services is a vital component of financial inclusion for individuals.

3. Financial Markets

3.1 Equity Markets

Equity markets are the best known of the financial markets and facilitate the trading of shares in quoted companies.

According to statistics from the World Federation of Exchanges (WFE), the total value of shares quoted on the world's stock exchanges was US$60 trillion at the end of 2014 (note: not all stock exchanges provide data to the WFE and so the actual figures may well be higher).

Market Capitalisation

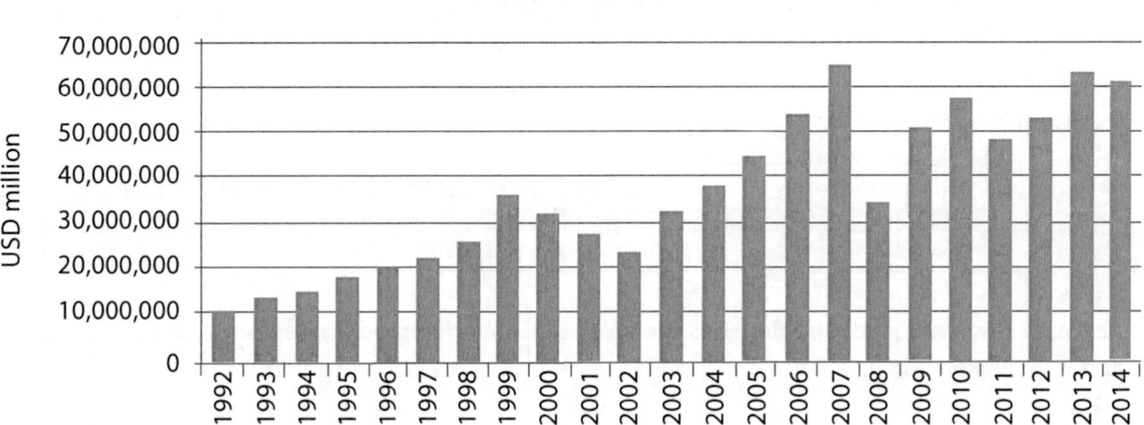

Source: World Federation of Exchanges

- The New York Stock Exchange (NYSE) is the largest exchange in the world and had a domestic market capitalisation of over US$19 trillion at the end of 2014 (domestic market capitalisation is the value of shares listed on an exchange).
- The other major US market, the National Association of Securities Dealers Automated Quotations system (NASDAQ), was ranked as the second largest with a domestic market capitalisation of nearly US$7 trillion, meaning that the two New York exchanges account for around one-third of all exchange business.
- The Tokyo Stock Exchange (TSE) is the world's third largest market and had a domestic market capitalisation of over US$4 trillion.
- In Europe, the largest exchanges are the London Stock Exchange (LSE), Euronext, Deutsche Börse, SIX Swiss Exchange and the Spanish exchanges.

Rivals to traditional stock exchanges have also arisen with the development of technology and communication networks known as **multilateral trading facilities (MTFs)**. These are systems that bring together multiple parties that are interested in buying and selling financial instruments, including shares, bonds and derivatives. These systems can be crossing networks or matching engines that are operated by an investment firm or another market operator.

We will look in more detail at equities and equity markets in Chapter 4.

3.2 Bond Markets

Although less well-known than equity markets, bond markets are larger both in size and value of trading. However, the volume of bond trading is lower, as most trades tend to be very large when compared to equity market trades.

The amounts outstanding on the global bond market now exceed US$100 trillion. Domestic bond markets account for around 70% of the total, and international bonds for the remainder. The bonds traded range from domestic bonds issued by companies and governments, to international bonds issued by companies, governments, and supranational agencies such as the World Bank. The US has the largest bond market, but trading in international bonds is predominantly undertaken in European markets.

3.3 Foreign Exchange Markets

Foreign exchange markets are the largest of all financial markets, with average daily turnover in excess of US$5 trillion.

The strength of one currency in relation to another and the rate at which one currency is exchanged for another is set by supply and demand. For example, if there is strong demand from Japanese investors for US dollars, the US dollar will rise in value relative to the Japanese yen.

There is an active foreign exchange market that enables governments, companies and individuals to deal with their cash inflows and outflows denominated in overseas currencies. The market is provided by the major banks, who each provide rates of exchange at which they are willing to buy or sell currencies. Historically, most foreign exchange deals were arranged over the telephone. Now, however, electronic trading is becoming increasingly prevalent.

Because foreign exchange is an OTC (over-the-counter) market, meaning one where brokers/dealers negotiate directly with one another, there is no central exchange or clearing house. Foreign exchange (also referred to as forex or just FX) trading is concentrated in a small number of financial centres.

The Bank for International Settlements (BIS) releases figures on the composition of the foreign exchange market every three years. The latest report for 2013 shows that market activity has become ever more concentrated in a handful of global centres. As you can see in the chart below, FX transactions are concentrated in five countries, with the UK as the main global centre.

Main Countries for FX Trading 2013

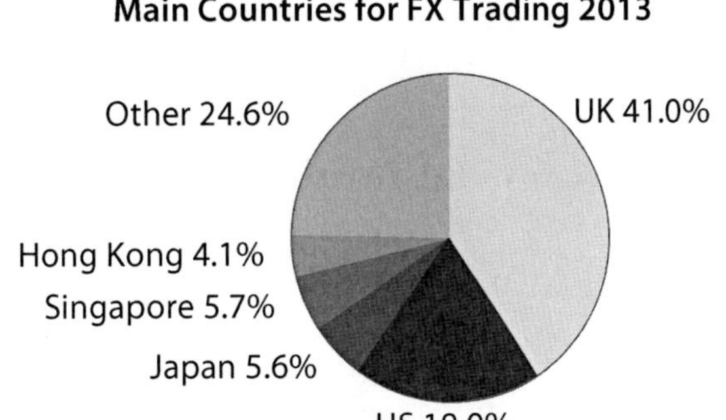

Source: *Bank for International Settlements*

3.4 Derivatives Markets

Derivatives markets trade a range of complex products based on underlying instruments, including currencies, indices, interest rates, equities, commodities and credit risk.

Derivatives based on these underlying elements are available on both the **exchange-traded** market and the **OTC** market. The largest of the exchange-traded derivatives markets is the Chicago Mercantile Exchange (CME), while Europe dominates trading in the OTC derivatives markets worldwide. Based on the value of the notional amounts outstanding, the OTC derivatives markets worldwide are about four times the size of stock quoted on stock exchanges.

Interest rate derivatives contracts account for three-quarters of outstanding derivatives contracts, mostly through interest rate swaps. In terms of currencies, the interest rate derivatives market is dominated by the euro and the US dollar, which have accounted for most of the growth in this market since 2001. The growth in the market came about as a reaction to the 2000–2002 stock market crash as traders sought to hedge their position against interest rate risk.

The UK enjoys the largest share of OTC foreign exchange derivatives turnover. After the UK, the US, Japan and Singapore are the next largest markets for foreign exchange derivatives, ahead of Germany, Hong Kong, Switzerland and Australia.

We will look in more detail at derivatives in Chapter 6.

3.5 Insurance Markets

Insurance markets specialise in the management of personal risk, corporate risk and protection of life events.

Globally, the US, Japan and the UK are the largest insurance markets, accounting for around 50% of worldwide premium income.

The market is led by a number of major players who dominate insurance activity in their market or regionally. These include well-known household names such as AIG (American International Group), AXA and Zurich Insurance.

4. Industry Participants

Learning Objective

1.1.1 Know the role of the following within the financial services industry: retail/commercial banks; savings institutions; investment banks; private banks; retirement schemes; insurance companies; fund managers; stockbrokers; custodians; third party administrators (TPAs); industry trade bodies; sovereign wealth funds

The number of organisations operating in the financial services industry is wide and varied. Each carries out a specialised function, and an understanding of their roles is important in order to understand how the industry is organised and how participants interact.

Although each participant is described as a separate organisation in the following sections, the nature of financial conglomerates means that some of the largest global firms may have divisions carrying out each of these activities.

4.1 Investment Banks

Investment banks provide advice and arrange finance for companies that want to float on the stock market, raise additional finance by issuing further shares or bonds, or carry out mergers and acquisitions. They also provide services for institutional firms that might want to invest in shares and bonds, in particular pension funds and asset managers.

Typically, an investment banking group provides some or all of the following services:

- Finance-raising and advisory work, both for governments and for companies. For corporate clients, this is normally in connection with new issues of securities to raise capital, as well as giving advice on mergers and acquisitions.
- Securities-trading in equities, bonds and derivatives and the provision of broking and distribution facilities.
- Treasury dealing for corporate clients in currencies, including 'financial engineering' services to protect them from interest rate and exchange rate fluctuations.
- Investment management for sizeable investors, such as corporate pension funds, charities and very wealthy private clients. In the larger investment banks, the value of funds under management runs into many billions of dollars.

Only a small number of investment banks provide services in all these areas. Most others tend to specialise to some degree and concentrate on only a few product lines. A number of banks have diversified their range of activities by developing businesses such as proprietary trading, servicing hedge funds, or making private equity investments.

4.2 Custodian Banks

Custodians are banks that specialise in safe custody services, looking after portfolios of shares and bonds on behalf of others, such as fund managers, pension funds and insurance companies. Activities they undertake include:

- Holding assets in safekeeping, such as equities and bonds.
- Arranging settlement of any purchases and sales of securities.
- Asset servicing – collecting income from assets, namely dividends in the case of equities and interest in the case of bonds, and processing corporate actions.
- Providing information on the underlying companies and their annual general meetings.
- Managing cash transactions.
- Performing foreign exchange transactions when required.
- Providing regular reporting on all activities undertaken that affect the holdings in a portfolio, including all trades, corporate actions and other transactions.

Cost pressures have driven down the charges that a custodian can make for its traditional custody services and have resulted in consolidation within the industry. The custody business is now dominated by a small number of **global custodians** who are often divisions of major banks. Among the biggest global custodians are the Bank of New York Mellon and State Street.

Generally, they also offer other services to their clients, such as stock lending, measuring the performance of the portfolios of which they have custody and maximising the return on any surplus cash.

4.3 Retail/Commercial Banks

Retail/commercial banks provide services such as taking deposits from, and lending funds to, retail customers, as well as providing payment and money transmission services. They may also provide similar services to business customers.

Historically these banks have tended to operate through a network of branches located on the high street, but increasingly they also provide internet and telephone banking services.

4.4 Savings Institutions

As well as retail banks, most countries also have savings institutions that started off by specialising in offering savings products to retail customers, but now tend to offer a similar range of services to those offered by banks.

They are known by different names around the world, such as *cajas* in Spanish-speaking countries, credit unions in North America and building societies in the UK. They are typically jointly owned by the individuals that have deposited or borrowed money from them – the members. It is for this reason that such savings organisations are often described as 'mutual societies'.

Over the years, many savings institutions have merged or been taken over by larger ones. More recently, a number have transformed themselves into banks that are quoted on stock exchanges – a process known as **demutualisation**.

4.5 Insurance Companies

As mentioned above, one of the key functions of the financial services industry is to allow risks to be managed effectively.

The insurance industry provides solutions for much more than the standard areas, such as life cover and general insurance cover.

Protection planning is a key area of financial advice, and the insurance industry provides a variety of products to meet many potential scenarios. These products range from payment protection policies designed to pay out in the event that an individual is unable to meet repayments on loans and mortgages, to fleet insurance against the risk of an airline's planes crashing.

Insurance companies collect premiums in exchange for the coverage provided. This premium income is invested in equities and bonds and, as a result, the insurance industry is a major investor in both equity and bond markets. Insurance companies will also hold a large amount of cash to be able to satisfy any claims that may arise on the various policies and, if required, will liquidate investment holdings.

4.6 Retirement Schemes

Retirement schemes (or pension schemes) are one of the key methods by which individuals can make provision for their retirement needs. There are a variety of retirement schemes available, ranging from ones provided by employers, to self-directed schemes.

Traditionally, company pension schemes provided an amount based on the employee's **final salary** and number of years of service. Nowadays most companies find this too expensive a commitment, given rising life-expectancy and volatile stock market returns. Most companies offer new staff **defined contribution schemes**, when both the firm and the employee contribute to an investment pot. At retirement, the accumulated fund is used to pay a pension.

Over the last 20 years or so, many individuals have opted to provide for their retirement through their own personal retirement schemes (self-directed schemes), perhaps opting out of schemes available from their employer.

Taken overall, retirement schemes are large, long-term investors in shares, bonds and cash. Some also invest in physical assets like property. To meet their aim of providing a pension on retirement, the sums of money invested in pensions are substantial.

4.7 Fund Managers

Fund managers, also known as investment managers, portfolio managers or asset managers, run portfolios of investments for others. They invest money held by institutions, such as pension funds and insurance companies, as well as wealthier individuals. Some are organisations that focus solely on this activity; others are divisions of larger entities, such as insurance companies or banks. Fund management is also known as asset management.

Investment managers will buy and sell shares, bonds and other assets in order to increase the value of their clients' portfolios. They can be subdivided into institutional and private client fund managers. Institutional fund managers work on behalf of institutions, for example, investing money for a company's pension fund or an insurance company's fund, or managing the investments of a mutual fund. Private client managers invest the money of relatively wealthy individuals. Obviously, institutional portfolios tend to be larger than those of regular private clients.

Fund managers charge their clients for managing their money. Their charges are often based on a small percentage of the value of the fund being managed.

Other areas of asset management include running so-called hedge funds and the provision of investment management services to institutional entities, such as charities and local government authorities.

4.8 Stockbrokers

Stockbrokers arrange stock market trades on behalf of their clients, who are investment institutions, fund managers or private investors. They may advise investors about which shares, funds or bonds they should buy or, alternatively, they may offer execution-only services, when the broker executes a trade on a client's instruction without providing advice. Many stockbrokers now offer wealth management services to their clients and so are also referred to as wealth managers.

Like fund managers, firms of stockbrokers can be independent companies, but some are divisions of larger entities, such as banks. They earn their profits by charging fees for their advice, and commission on transactions.

Also like fund managers, stockbrokers look after client assets and charge custody and portfolio management fees.

4.9 Private Banks

Private banks provide a wide range of services for their clients, including wealth management, estate planning, tax planning, insurance, lending and lines of credit. Their services are normally targeted at clients with a certain minimum sum of investable cash, or minimum net worth. These clients are generally referred to as **high net worth individuals**.

Private banking is offered both by domestic banks and by those operating 'offshore'. In this context, offshore banking means banking in a jurisdiction different from the client's home country – usually one with a favourable tax regime.

Competition in private banking has expanded in recent years as the number of banks providing private banking services has increased dramatically. The private banking market is relatively fragmented, with many medium-sized and small players.

The distinction between private and retail banks is gradually diminishing as private banks reduce their investment thresholds in order to compete for this market; meanwhile, many high street banks are also expanding their services to attract the 'mass affluent' and high net worth individuals.

4.10 Sovereign Wealth Funds

A sovereign wealth fund (SWF) is a state-owned investment fund that holds financial assets such as equities, bonds, real estate, or other financial instruments. Examples of SWFs include the Norway Government Pension Fund, Abu Dhabi Investment Authority, SAMA Foreign Holdings of Saudi Arabia and China Investment Corporation.

SWFs are defined as special purpose investment funds or arrangements owned by a government. Their key characteristics are:

- SWFs hold, manage, or administer assets to achieve financial objectives.
- They employ a set of investment strategies which include investing in foreign financial assets.
- The assets of an SWF are commonly established out of balance of payments surpluses, official foreign currency operations, the proceeds of privatisations, fiscal surpluses, and receipts resulting from commodity exports.

Sovereign wealth funds have emerged as major investors in the global markets over the last ten years, but they date back at least five decades to the surpluses built up by oil-producing countries and, more recently, to the trade surpluses that countries such as China have enjoyed.

Sovereign wealth funds have colossal funds under management and are predicted to grow beyond the US$10 trillion mark within a few years as the investment flows from East to West intensify.

They are private investment vehicles that have varied and undisclosed investment objectives. Typically, their primary focus is on well-above-average returns from investments made abroad. Their size and global diversification allows them to participate in the best opportunities, spread their risks and, by diverting their funds overseas, prevent the overheating of their local economies. They may also use part of their wealth as reserve capital for when their countries' natural resources are depleted.

For some of the wealthiest SWFs, it should be noted that the term 'sovereign' is not synonymous with public ownership.

SWFs are becoming increasingly important in the international monetary and financial system, attracting growing attention. This growth has also raised several issues:

- Official and private commentators have expressed concerns about the transparency of SWFs, including their size and their investment strategies, and that SWF investments may be affected by political objectives.
- There are also concerns about how their investments might affect recipient countries, leading to talk about protectionist restrictions on their investments, which could hamper the international flow of capital.

In response to these concerns, the International Working Group of Sovereign Wealth Funds (IWG) has been formed and has published a set of 24 voluntary principles, the Generally Accepted Principles and Practices for Sovereign Wealth Funds, known as the Santiago Principles. This is leading to increasing transparency, with a number of countries now publishing annual reports and disclosing their assets under management.

4.11 Trade Bodies

The investment industry is a dynamic, rapidly changing business, and one that requires co-operation between firms to ensure that the views of various industry sections are represented, especially to governments and regulators, and that cross-firm developments can take place to create an efficient market in which those firms can operate.

This is the role of the numerous trade bodies that exist across the world's financial markets. Examples of these that operate globally are the **International Capital Market Association (ICMA)**, which concentrates on international bond dealing, and the **International Swaps and Derivatives Association (ISDA)**, which produces standards that firms that operate in derivatives markets follow when dealing with each other.

4.12 Third Party Administrators

Third party administrators (TPAs) undertake investment administration on behalf of other firms, and specialise in this area of the investment industry.

The number of firms, and the scale of their operations, has grown with the increasing use of **outsourcing** by firms. The rationale behind outsourcing has been that it enables a firm to focus on the core areas of its business (for example, investment management and stock selection, or the provision of appropriate financial planning) and leave another firm to carry on the administrative functions which it can process more efficiently.

End of Chapter Questions

Think of an answer for each question and refer to the appropriate section for confirmation.

1. What are the main types of services provided by investment banks?
   Answer Reference: Section 4.1

2. What services does a custodian offer?
   Answer Reference: Section 4.2

3. How does a mutual savings institution differ from a retail bank?
   Answer Reference: Sections 4.3 and 4.4

4. What is protection planning and what scenarios can protection policies provide cover for?
   Answer Reference: Section 4.5

5. What sectors of the financial services industry do ICMA and ISDA represent?
   Answer Reference: Section 4.11

6. What is the role of a third party administrator?
   Answer Reference: Section 4.12

Chapter Two

The Economic Environment

This syllabus area will provide approximately 3 of the 50 examination questions

1. Introduction

In this chapter we turn to the broader economic environment in which the financial services industry operates.

First, we will look at how economic activity is determined in various economic and political systems, and then look at the role of governments and central banks in the management of that economic activity.

Finally, the chapter concludes with an explanation of some of the key economic measures that provide an indication of the state of an economy.

2. Factors Determining Economic Activity

Learning Objective

2.1.1 Know the factors which determine the level of economic activity: state-controlled economies; market economies; mixed economies; open economies

2.1 State-Controlled Economies

A state-controlled economy is one in which the state (in the form of the government) decides what is produced and how it is distributed. The best known example of a state-controlled economy was the Soviet Union throughout most of the 20th century.

Sometimes these economies are referred to as **planned economies**, because the production and allocation of resources is planned in advance rather than allowed to respond to market forces. However, the need for careful planning and control can bring about excessive layers of bureaucracy, and state control inevitably removes a great deal of individual choice.

These factors have contributed to the reform of the economies of the former Soviet states and the introduction of a more mixed economy (covered in more detail in Section 2.3).

2.2 Market Economies

In a market economy, the forces of supply and demand determine how resources are allocated.

Businesses produce goods and services to meet the demand from consumers. The interaction of demand from consumers and supply from businesses in the market will result in the market-clearing price – the price that reflects the balance between what consumers will willingly pay for goods and services, and what suppliers will willingly accept for them.

If there is oversupply, the price will be low and some producers will leave the market. If there is undersupply, the price will be high, attracting new producers into the market.

There is a market not only for goods and services, but also for productive assets, such as capital goods (eg, machinery), labour and money. For the labour market, it is the wage level that is effectively the 'price', and for the money market it is the interest rate.

People compete for jobs and companies compete for customers in a market economy. Scarce resources, including skilled labour, such as that provided by a football player, or a financial asset, such as a share in a successful company, will have a high value. In a market economy, competition means that inferior football players and shares in unsuccessful companies will be much cheaper and, ultimately, competition could bring about the collapse of the unsuccessful company, and result in the inferior football player seeking an alternative career.

2.3 Mixed Economies

A mixed economy combines a market economy with some element of state control. The vast majority of established markets operate as mixed economies to a lesser or greater extent.

While most of us would agree that unsuccessful companies should be allowed to fail, we generally feel that the less able in society should be cushioned from the full force of the market economy.

In a mixed economy, the government will provide a welfare system to support the unemployed, the infirm and the elderly, in tandem with the market-driven aspects of the economy. Governments will also spend money running key areas such as defence, education, public transport, health and police services.

Governments raise finance for this public expenditure by:

- collecting taxes directly from wage-earners and companies;
- collecting indirect taxes (eg, sales tax and taxes on petrol, cigarettes and alcohol); and
- raising money through borrowing in the capital markets.

2.4 Open Economies

In an open economy there are few barriers to trade or controls over foreign exchange.

Although most western governments create barriers to protect their citizens against illegal drugs and other dangers, they generally have policies to allow or encourage free trade.

From time to time, issues will arise when one country believes another is taking unfair advantage of trade policies and will take some form of retaliatory action, possibly including the imposition of sanctions. When a country prevents other countries from trading freely with it in order to preserve its domestic market, this is usually referred to as **protectionism**.

The World Trade Organisation (WTO) exists to promote the growth of free trade between economies. It is, therefore, sometimes called upon to arbitrate when disputes arise.

3. Central Banks

Traditionally, the role of government has been to manage the economy through taxation and economic and monetary policy, and to ensure a fair society by the state provision of welfare and benefits to those who meet certain criteria, while leaving businesses relatively free to address the challenges and opportunities that arise.

Governments can use a variety of policies when attempting to reduce the impact of fluctuations in economic activity. Collectively these measures are known as **stabilisation policies** and are categorised under the broad headings of **fiscal policy** and **monetary policy**. Fiscal policy involves making adjustments using government spending and taxation, while monetary policy involves making adjustments to interest rates and the money supply.

Rather than following either one or the other type of policy, most governments now adopt a pragmatic approach to controlling the level of economic activity through a combination of fiscal and monetary policy. In an increasingly integrated world, however, controlling the level of activity in an open economy in isolation is difficult, as financial markets, rather than individual governments and central banks, tend to dictate economic policy.

Governments implement their monetary policies using their central bank, and a consideration of their role in this implementation is noted below.

3.1 The Role of Central Banks

Learning Objective

2.1.2 Know the role of central banks

Central banks operate at the very centre of a nation's financial system. They are public bodies but, increasingly, they operate independently of government control or political interference. They usually have the following responsibilities:

- Acting as banker to the banking system by accepting deposits from, and lending to, commercial banks.
- Acting as banker to the government.
- Managing the national debt.
- Regulating the domestic banking system.
- Acting as lender of last resort to the banking system in financial crises to prevent the systemic collapse of the banking system.
- Setting the official short-term rate of interest.
- Controlling the money supply.
- Issuing notes and coins.
- Holding the nation's gold and foreign currency reserves.
- Influencing the value of a nation's currency through activities such as intervention in the currency markets.
- Providing a depositors' protection scheme for bank deposits.

The table below shows details of some of the world's main central banks.

Federal Reserve (the Fed)	• The Federal Reserve System in the US dates back to 1913. The Fed, as it is known, comprises 12 regional Federal Reserve Banks, each of which monitors the activities of, and provides liquidity to, the banks in its region. • The Federal Open Market Committee (FOMC) takes responsibility for decisions, which are directed towards its statutory duty of promoting price stability and sustainable economic growth. • The FOMC meets every six weeks or so to examine the latest economic data in order to gauge the health of the economy and determine whether the economically sensitive Fed funds rate should be altered. Very occasionally it meets in emergency session, if economic circumstances dictate. • As lender of last resort to the US banking system, the Fed has, in recent years, rescued a number of US financial institutions and markets from collapse. In doing so it has prevented widespread panic, and prevented systemic risk from spreading throughout the financial system.
European Central Bank (ECB)	• The ECB is based in Frankfurt. It assumed its central banking responsibilities upon the creation of the euro, on 1 January 1999. • It is principally responsible for setting monetary policy for the entire eurozone, with the sole objective of maintaining internal price stability. Its objective of keeping inflation, as defined by the harmonised index of consumer prices (HICP), *'close to but below 2% in the medium term'* is achieved by influencing those factors that may influence inflation, such as the external value of the euro and growth in the money supply. • The ECB sets its monetary policy through its president and council, the latter of which comprises the governors of each of the eurozone's national central banks.
Bank of England (BoE)	• The UK's central bank, the BoE, was founded in 1694, but it wasn't until 1997, when the BoE's Monetary Policy Committee (MPC) was established, that the Bank gained operational independence in setting UK monetary policy, in line with that of most other developed nations. • The MPC's primary focus is to ensure that inflation is kept within a government-set range. It does this by setting the base rate, an officially published short-term interest rate and the MPC's sole policy instrument. • In addition to its short-term interest rate-setting role, the BoE also assumes responsibility for all other traditional central bank activities, with the exception of managing the national debt and providing a depositors' protection scheme for bank deposits.
Bank of Japan (BoJ)	• The BoJ began operating as Japan's central bank in 1882 and, like the BoE, gained operational independence in 1997. • The Bank is responsible for the country's monetary policy, issuing and managing the external value of the Japanese yen, and acting as lender of last resort to the Japanese banking system.

4. Inflation

In this next section we look at the impact of inflation. We will look first at how goods and services are paid for and how credit is created, and then at its interaction with inflation.

4.1 Credit Creation

Learning Objective

2.1.3 Know how goods and services are paid for and how credit is created

Most of what we buy is not paid for using cash. We find it more convenient to pay by card or cheque.

It is fairly easy (subject to the borrower's credit status) to buy something now and pay later, for example by going overdrawn, using a credit card or taking out a loan. Loans will often be for more substantial purchases, such as a house or a car. Buying now and paying later is generally referred to as purchasing goods and services 'on credit'.

The banking system provides a mechanism by which credit can be created. This means that banks can increase the total money supply in the economy.

Example

New Bank sets up business and is granted a banking licence. It is authorised to take deposits and make loans. Because New Bank knows that only a small proportion of the deposited funds are likely to be demanded at any one time, it will be able to lend the deposited money to others. New Bank will make profits by lending money out at a higher rate than it pays depositors. These loans provide an increase in the money supply in circulation – New Bank is creating credit.

By this action of lending to borrowers, banks create money and advance this to industry, consumers and governments. This money circulates within the economy, being spent on goods and services by the people who have borrowed it from the banks. The people to whom it is paid (the providers of those goods and services) will then deposit it in their own bank accounts, allowing the banks to use it to create fresh credit all over again.

It is estimated that this credit creation process accounts for 96% of the money in circulation in most industrialised nations, with only 4% being in the form of notes and coins created by the government. If this process were uncontrolled, it would lead to a rapid increase in the money supply and, with too much money chasing too few goods, to an increase in inflation.

Understandably, therefore, central banks aim to keep the amount of credit creation under control as part of their overall monetary policy. They will aim to ensure that the amount of credit creation is below the level at which it would increase the money supply so much that inflation accelerates. A central bank will do this through changes to interest rates in order to influence demand for loans: when interest rates are high, people borrow less; when rates are low, the opportunity cost of leaving the money in the bank is lower, so people will spend. The cost of borrowing to spend is also lower, so people will spend more, or make larger purchases. A central bank will also influence demand through the level of reserves that banks are required to maintain with the central bank, in order to affect the supply of credit.

4.2 The Impact of Inflation

Learning Objective

2.1.4 Understand the meaning of inflation: measurement; impact; control

Inflation is a persistent increase in the general level of prices. There are a number of reasons for prices to increase, such as excess demand in the economy, scarcity of resources and key workers or rapidly increasing government spending. Most western governments seek to control inflation at a level of about 2–3% per annum – not letting it get too high (or too low).

High levels of inflation can cause problems:

- Businesses have to continually update prices to keep pace with inflation.
- Employees find the real value of their salaries eroded.
- Those on fixed levels of income, such as pensioners, will suffer as the price increases are not matched by increases in income.
- Exports may become less competitive.
- The real value of future pensions and investment income becomes difficult to assess, which might act as a disincentive to save.

There are, however, some positive aspects to high levels of inflation:

- Rising house prices contribute to a 'feel-good' factor (although this might contribute to further inflation as house owners become more eager to borrow and spend and lead to unsustainable rises in prices and a subsequent crash, as has been seen recently).
- Borrowers benefit, because the value of borrowers' debt falls in real terms – ie, after adjusting for the effect of inflation.
- Inflation also erodes the real value of a country's national debt and so can benefit an economy in difficult times.

Central banks use interest rates to control inflation. They set an interest rate at which they will lend to financial institutions, and this influences the rates that are available to savers and borrowers. The result is that movements in base rate affect spending by companies and their customers and, over time, the rate of inflation.

Changes in base rate can take up to two years to have their full impact on inflation, so the central bank has to look ahead when deciding on the appropriate monetary policy. If inflation looks set to rise above target, then the central bank raises rates to slow spending and reduce inflation. Similarly, if inflation looks set to fall below its target level, it reduces bank rates to boost spending and inflation.

As well as experiencing inflation, economies can also face the problems presented by **deflation**. Deflation is defined as a general fall in price levels. Although not experienced as a worldwide phenomenon since the 1930s, deflation has been seen in an increasing number of countries.

Deflation typically results from negative demand shocks, such as the bursting of the 1990s technology bubble, and from excess capacity and production. It creates a vicious circle of reduced spending and a reluctance to borrow as the real burden of debt increases in an environment of falling prices.

It should be noted that falling prices are not necessarily a destructive force per se and, indeed, can be beneficial if they are as a result of positive supply shocks, such as rising productivity growth and greater price competition caused by the globalisation of the world economy and increased price transparency.

There are various measures of inflation, but the most common term encountered is the consumer price index (CPI).

In Europe, for example, the main measure is the **CPI**. This is also known as the **HICP** and is a measure of inflation that is prepared in a standard way throughout the European Union. It excludes mortgage interest payments, mostly because a large proportion of the population in continental Europe rent their homes, rather than buying them.

Most countries measure inflation in a similar way to Europe, with the majority using the term 'CPI' for their index, although there are some differences in how it is calculated. The advantage of a common way of measuring inflation is where it needs to be compared on a like-for-like basis with other countries.

It is important to recognise, however, that there are different ways of calculating inflation, and that different measures may give alternative pictures of what is happening in the real global economy.

4.3 Measures of Economic Data

Learning Objective

2.1.5 Understand the impact of the following economic data: gross domestic product (GDP); balance of payments; level of unemployment

In addition to inflation measures like the CPI, there are a number of other economic statistics carefully watched by governments and by other market participants as potentially significant indicators of how economies are performing.

4.3.1 Gross Domestic Product (GDP)

At the very simplest level, an economy comprises two distinct groups: individuals and firms. Individuals supply firms with the productive resources of the economy in exchange for an income. In turn, these individuals use this income to buy the entire output produced by firms employing these resources. This gives rise to what is known as the **circular flow of income**.

Simplified Model of the Economy

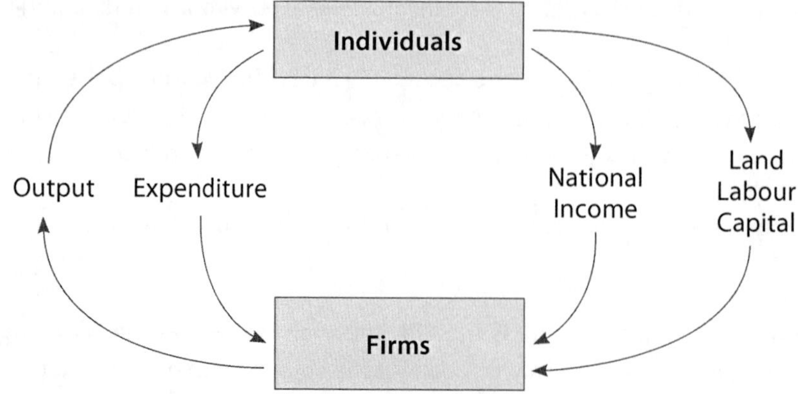

This economic activity can be measured in one of three ways:

- by the total income paid by firms to individuals;
- by individuals' total expenditure on firms' output; or
- by the value of total output generated by firms.

GDP is the most commonly used measure of a country's output. It measures economic activity on an expenditure basis and is typically calculated quarterly as follows:

Gross Domestic Product	
	consumer spending
plus	government spending
plus	investment
plus	exports
less	imports
equals	GDP

Economic Growth

There are many sources from which economic growth can emanate, but in the long run the rate of sustainable growth (or **trend rate of growth**) ultimately depends on:

- the growth and productivity of the labour force;
- the rate at which an economy efficiently channels its domestic savings and capital attracted from overseas into new and innovative technology and replaces obsolescent capital equipment;
- the extent to which an economy's infrastructure is maintained and developed to cope with growing transport, communication and energy needs.

In a mature economy, the labour force typically grows at about 1% per annum, though in countries such as the US, where immigrant labour is increasingly employed, the annual growth rate has been in excess of this. Long-term productivity growth is dependent on factors such as education and training and the utilisation of labour-saving new technology. Moreover, productivity gains are more difficult to extract in a post-industrialised economy than in one with a large manufacturing base.

Given these factors, the US's long-term trend rate of economic growth has averaged nearly 3%. In developing economies, however, economic growth rates of up to 10% per annum are not uncommon.

The fact that actual growth fluctuates and deviates from trend growth in the short term gives rise to the **economic cycle**, or business cycle.

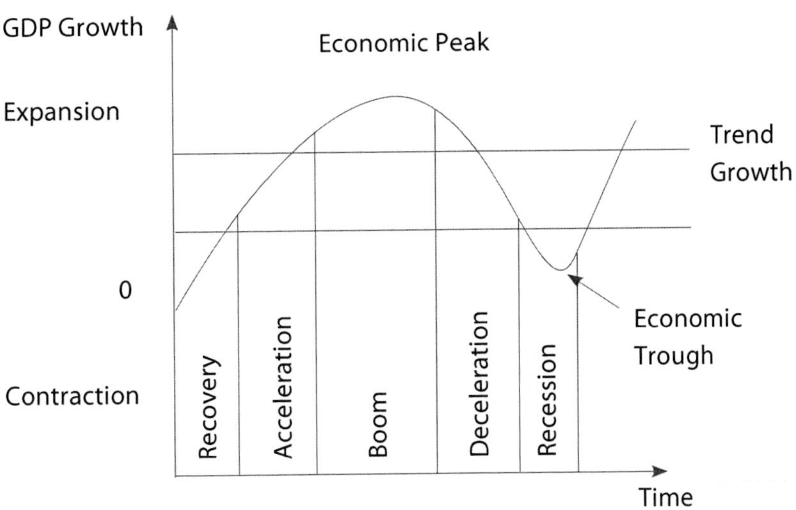

When an economy is growing in excess of its trend growth rate, actual output will exceed potential output, often with inflationary consequences. However, when a country's output contracts – that is, when its economic growth rate turns negative for at least two consecutive calendar quarters – the economy is said to be in recession, or entering a deflationary period, resulting in spare capacity and unemployment.

4.3.2 Balance of Payments

The balance of payments is a summary of all the transactions between a country and the rest of the world. If the country imports more than it exports, there is a **balance of payments deficit**. If the country exports more than it imports, there is a **balance of payments surplus**.

The main components of the balance of payments are the trade balance, the current account and the capital account.

<table>
<tr><td>Trade Balance</td><td><ul><li>The trade balance comprises:<ul><li>a visible trade balance – the difference between the value of imported and exported goods, such as those arising from the trade of raw materials and manufactured goods;</li><li>and an invisible trade balance – the difference between the value of imported and exported services, arising from services such as banking, financial services and tourism.</li></ul></li><li>If a country has a trade deficit in one of these areas or overall, this means that it imports more than it exports, and if it has a trade surplus, it exports more than it imports.</li></ul></td></tr>
<tr><td>Current Account</td><td><ul><li>The current account is used to calculate the total value of goods and services that flow into and out of a country.</li><li>The current account comprises the trade balance figures for the visibles and invisibles.</li><li>To these figures are added other receipts, such as dividends from overseas assets and remittances from nationals working abroad.</li></ul></td></tr>
<tr><td>Capital Account</td><td><ul><li>The capital account records international capital transactions related to investment in business, real estate, bonds and stocks. This includes transactions relating to the ownership of fixed assets and the purchase and sale of domestic and foreign investment assets.</li><li>These are usually divided into categories such as foreign direct investment, when an overseas firm acquires a new plant or an existing business, portfolio investment which includes trading in stocks and bonds, and other investments, which include transactions in currency and bank deposits.</li></ul></td></tr>
</table>

For the balance of payments to balance, the current account must equal the capital account plus or minus a balancing item – used to rectify the many errors in compiling the balance of payments – plus or minus any change in central bank foreign currency reserves.

A current account deficit resulting from a country being a net importer of overseas goods and services must be met by a net inflow of capital from overseas, taking account of any measurement errors and any central bank intervention in the foreign currency market.

Having the 'right' **exchange rate** is critical to the level of international trade undertaken, to international competitiveness and therefore to a country's economic position. This can be understood by looking at what happens if a country's exchange rate alters.

If the value of its currency rises, then exports will be less competitive, unless producers reduce their prices, and imports will be cheaper and therefore more competitive. The result will be either to reduce a trade surplus or worsen a trade deficit.

If its value falls against other currencies then the reverse happens: exports will be cheaper in foreign markets and so more competitive, and imports will be more expensive and therefore less competitive. A trade surplus or deficit will therefore see an improving position.

4.3.3 Level of Unemployment

The extent to which those seeking employment cannot find work is an important indicator of the health of the economy. There is always likely to be some unemployment in an economy – certain people are in the process of looking for a new job that better suits them, or they are returning to the workforce after some time off, or they could be new immigrants, or lacking the right skills, or are living in areas in which it is difficult to find work. Higher levels of unemployment indicate low demand in the economy for goods and services produced and sold to consumers and, therefore, low demand for people to provide them.

High unemployment levels will have a negative impact on a government's finances. The government will need to increase social security/welfare payments, and its income will decrease because of the lack of tax revenues from the unemployed.

End of Chapter Questions

Think of an answer for each question and refer to the appropriate section for confirmation.

1. What are the key differences between state-controlled and market economies?
   Answer Reference: Sections 2.1 & 2.2

2. Which international organisation has the role of reducing trade barriers?
   Answer Reference: Section 2.4

3. What are the main functions of a central bank?
   Answer Reference: Section 3.1

4. What would be the effect of uncontrolled growth in the money supply?
   Answer Reference: Section 4.1

5. What are the negative effects of inflation?
   Answer Reference: Section 4.2

6. What economic measure is used as an indicator of the health of the economy?
   Answer Reference: Section 4.3.1

7. What does the balance of payments represent?
   Answer Reference: Section 4.3.2

8. What is the impact of high unemployment levels on the economy?
   Answer Reference: Section 4.3.3

Chapter Three

Financial Assets and Markets

This syllabus area will provide approximately 7 of the 50 examination questions

1. Introduction

This chapter provides an overview of the main asset classes and then looks particularly at the money market, the property market and foreign exchange.

Subsequent chapters will look in more detail at equities, bonds and derivatives.

2. Asset Classes

In this section, we take an introductory look at the characteristics of the principal asset classes, namely cash, bonds, equities and property.

2.1 Cash Instruments

Nearly all investors keep at least part of their wealth in the form of cash, which will be deposited with a bank or other savings institution to earn interest. Cash investments take two main forms: cash deposits and money market instruments.

2.1.1 Cash Deposits

Learning Objective

3.1.1 Know the characteristics of fixed-term and instant access deposit accounts

3.1.2 Understand the distinction between gross and net interest payments

3.1.3 Be able to calculate the net interest due given the gross interest rate, the deposited sum, the period and tax rate

3.1.4 Know the advantages and disadvantages of investing in cash

---

Cash deposits comprise accounts held with banks or other savings institutions. They are held by a wide variety of depositors – from retail investors through to companies, governments and financial institutions.

The main characteristics of cash deposits are:

- The return simply comprises interest income with no potential for capital growth.
- The amount invested (the **capital**) is repaid in full at the end of the investment term.

The interest rate paid on deposits will also vary with the amount of money deposited and the time for which the money is tied up.

- Large deposits are more economical for a bank to process and will earn a better rate.

- Fixed-term accounts involve the investor tying up their money for a fixed period of time such as one, two or three years, or when a fixed period of notice has to be given such as 30 days, 60 days or 90 days. In exchange for tying up their funds for these periods, the investor will demand a higher rate of interest than would be available on accounts that permit immediate access.
- Instant access deposit accounts typically earn the lowest rates of interest of the various deposit accounts available.
- Current (US: checking) accounts will generate an even lower rate, and sometimes pay no interest at all.

Generally, interest received by an individual is subject to income tax. In many countries, tax is deducted at source – that is, by the deposit-taker before paying the interest to the depositor. The 'headline' rate of interest quoted by deposit-takers, before deduction of tax, is referred to as **gross interest**, and the rate of interest after tax is deducted is referred to as **net interest**.

For this exam, it is necessary to be able to calculate the net interest due, so study the example and then practice this using the two exercises. The answers to the exercises are at the end of this chapter.

Example

Mrs Jones is entitled to 5% gross interest on €200 deposited in XYZ Bank for a year, and tax at 20% is deducted before payment of the interest.

She will earn €200 x 5% = €10 interest on her bank deposit before the deduction of any tax. She will receive €8 from XYZ Bank. XYZ Bank will subsequently pay the €2 of tax on behalf of Mrs Jones to the tax authorities.

This can be summarised as follows:

Gross interest earned: €200 x 5% = €10.

Tax deducted by XYZ Bank: 20% x €10 = €2.

Net interest received by Mrs Jones: €10 x 80% = €8.

Exercise 1

Mr Evans pays tax at 20%, and all of the tax is deducted at source. He has had €3,000 on deposit at XYZ Bank for a year, earning 4% gross interest. How much interest does Mr Evans receive, and how much tax is deducted?

Exercise 2

Alan pays tax in his country at 20%. Alan has €10,000 on deposit at XYZ Bank earning 3% gross interest. What is the net rate of interest he is earning?

Exercise 3

Mrs Smith pays tax at 20%, all of which is deducted at source. She has had €10,000 on deposit at XYZ Bank for six months, earning 3% per annum gross interest. How much interest does Mrs Smith receive at the end of six months, and how much tax is deducted?

Advantages and Disadvantages

There are a number of **advantages** to investing in cash:

- One of the key reasons for holding money in the form of cash deposits is liquidity. Liquidity is the ease and speed with which an investment can be turned into cash to meet spending needs. Most investors are likely to have a need for cash at short notice and so should plan to hold some cash on deposit to meet possible needs and emergencies before considering other less liquid investments.
- The other main reasons for holding cash investments are as a savings vehicle and for the interest return that can be earned on them.
- A further advantage is the relative safety that cash investments have and that they are not exposed to market volatility, as is the case with other types of assets.

Investing in cash does have some serious **drawbacks**, however, including:

- Banks and savings institutions are of varying creditworthiness and the risk that they may default needs to be assessed and taken into account.
- Inflation reduces the real return that is being earned on cash deposits and often the after-tax return can be negative.
- Interest rates vary, and so the returns from cash-based deposits will also vary.
- During periods of low global interest rates, charges on money market funds can result in negative or flat returns.

Although banks and savings institutions are licensed, monitored and regulated, it is still possible that such institutions might fail, as has been seen recently in the aftermath of the financial crisis. Deposits are therefore usually also protected by a government-sponsored **compensation scheme**. This will repay any deposited money lost, typically up to a set maximum, due to the collapse of a bank or savings institution. The sum is generally fixed so as to be of meaningful protection to most retail investors, although it would be of less help to very substantial depositors.

When cash is deposited overseas, depositors should also consider the following:

- The costs of currency conversion and the potential exchange rate risks if the deposit is not made in the investor's home currency.
- The creditworthiness of the banking system and the chosen deposit-taking institution, and whether a depositors' protection scheme exists and if non-residents are protected under it. Not every country operates one, and so the onus is on the investor or their adviser to check.
- The tax treatment of interest applied to the deposit.
- Whether the deposit will be subject to any exchange controls that may restrict access to the money and its ultimate repatriation.

2.1.2 Money Markets

Learning Objective

3.2.1 Know the difference between a capital market instrument and a money market instrument

3.2.2 Know the definition and features of the following: Treasury bill; commercial paper; certificate of deposit

3.2.3 Know the advantages and disadvantages of investing in money market instruments

The **money markets** are the wholesale or institutional markets for cash and are characterised by the issue, trading and redemption of short-dated negotiable securities. These can have a maturity of up to one year, though three months or less is more typical.

By contrast, the **capital markets** are the long-term providers of finance for companies, either through investment in bonds or shares.

Owing to the short-term nature of the money markets, most instruments are issued at a discount to their face value to save on the administration associated with registration and the payment of interest. Although accessible to retail investors indirectly through collective investment (mutual) funds, direct investment in money market instruments is often subject to a relatively high minimum subscription and therefore tends to be more suitable for institutional investors.

Examples of the main types of money market instruments are shown below.

Treasury Bills	• **Treasury bills** – these are usually issued weekly by or on behalf of governments, and the money is used to meet the government's short-term borrowing needs. • Treasury bills are non-interest-bearing instruments and so are sometimes referred to as 'zero coupon' instruments (see Chapter 5, Section 4.2.5). • Instead of interest being paid out on them, they are issued at a discount to par – ie, a price of less than US$100 per US$100 nominal – and commonly redeemed after three months. For example, a Treasury bill might be issued for US$998 and mature at US$1,000 three months later. The investor's return is the difference between the US$998 they paid, and the US$1,000 they receive on the Treasury bill's maturity.
Certificates of Deposit	• **Certificates of deposit (CDs)** – these are issued by banks in return for deposited money: think of them as tradeable deposit accounts, as they can be bought and sold in the same way as shares. For example, ABC Bank might issue a CD to represent a deposit of US$1 million from a customer, redeemable in six months. The CD might specify that ABC Bank will pay the US$1 million back, plus interest of, say, 2.5% of US$1 million. If the customer needs the money back before six months has elapsed, they can sell the CD to another investor in the money market.

Commercial Paper	• **Commercial paper (CP)** – this is the corporate equivalent of a Treasury bill. Commercial paper is issued by large companies to meet their short-term borrowing needs. A company's ability to issue commercial paper is typically agreed with banks in advance. For example, a company might agree with its bank to a programme of US$10 million worth of commercial paper. This would enable the company to issue various forms of commercial paper with different maturities (eg, one month, three months and six months), and possibly different currencies, to the bank. As with Treasury bills, commercial paper is zero coupon and issued at a discount to its par value.

These money market instruments are all bearer instruments for which the issuer does not maintain a register of ownership. Ownership is simply evidenced by holding the instruments.

Settlement of money market instruments is typically achieved through the same settlement system that is used for equities and bonds, and is commonly settled on the day of the trade or the following business day.

As mentioned earlier, the money market is a highly professional market that is used by banks and companies to manage their liquidity needs. It is not readily accessible by private investors, who instead need to utilise either money market accounts offered by banks, or money market funds.

A **money market account** is perhaps better described as a money market deposit account. It is essentially a savings account that typically requires a substantial minimum balance and notice period. As it is a form of bank account, the depositor generally has the safety net of some form of depositor protection scheme.

In contrast, a **money market fund** is actually a money market mutual fund, a collective investment scheme which pools investors' money to invest in short-term debt instruments, such as Treasury bills and commercial paper. There is a range of money market funds available and they can offer two major advantages over money market accounts. An obvious advantage is the pooling of funds with other investors, which gives the investor access to assets they would not otherwise be able to invest in. The returns on money market funds tend to also be greater than a simple money market account offered by a bank, mainly because the investor is taking a greater risk since such funds are not covered by the depositor protection scheme.

Advantages and Disadvantages

Cash deposits provide a low-risk way to generate an income or capital return, as appropriate, while preserving the nominal value of the amount invested. They also play a valuable role in times of market uncertainty. However, they are unsuitable for anything other than the short term as, historically, they have underperformed most other asset types over the medium to long term. Moreover, in the long term, the return from cash deposits has often been barely positive after the effects of inflation and taxation are taken into account.

So, money market investments can be used instead to fulfil a number of roles within a client's portfolio, including:

- as a short-term home for cash balances;
- as an alternative to bonds and equities (particularly in uncertain times).

As seen, money market deposit accounts can be used as a temporary home for idle cash balances rather than using a standard retail deposit account. For the retail investor, these accounts can at times offer higher returns than can be achieved on standard deposits, and are offered by most retail banks.

The disadvantage is that the higher returns can usually only be achieved with relatively large investments. As an alternative, a money market fund can produce greater returns due to the pooled nature of this collective investment vehicle, which can access better rates than smaller deposits.

Money markets also offer a potentially safe haven in times of market falls. When markets have had a long bull period and economic prospects begin to worsen, an investor may want to take profits at the peak of the market cycle and invest the funds raised in the money markets until better investment opportunities arise.

The same rationale can be used when the investor does not want to commit new cash at the top of the market cycle. The nature of money market instruments means that they offer an alternative investment that gives limited exposure to any appreciable market risk.

Within a client's normal portfolio of investments, a proportion of the investments will be held as cash. Money market investments can therefore be the vehicle for holding such asset allocations, and are in competition with other short-term deposit accounts.

Money market funds, therefore, can have a core role to play in an investment portfolio. It does need to be remembered, however, that they still carry some risks, and the level of risk varies between one type of instrument and another. The short-term nature of the money market instruments provides some protection, but short-term interest rates fluctuate frequently, which will result in some price volatility.

2.2 Bonds

It is impossible to consider asset classes without looking at bonds. Below is a brief description of bonds. These will be more fully covered later in this workbook, in Chapter 5.

Bonds are essentially IOUs – the issuer of the bond receives money from the initial buyer of the bond and undertakes to pay the holder of the bond regular interest, and then return the money (the capital) at a particular future date.

Although bonds rarely generate as much comment as shares, they are the larger market of the two in terms of global investment value. Bonds are roughly equally split between government and corporate bonds.

- **Government bonds** are issued by national governments (eg, Japan, the US, Italy, Germany, and the UK).
- **Supranational bonds** are issued by agencies, such as the European Investment Bank and the World Bank.
- **Corporate bonds** are issued by companies, such as large banks and other large listed companies.

Bonds are generally less risky than shares, providing that their issuers remain solvent. Investments such as government bonds have until recently been regarded as being of particularly low risk, as it has been regarded as unlikely that a government will default, ie, fail to pay the interest or repay the capital on the bond (although it has happened, usually when a country undergoes a turbulent regime change or serious economic problems such as are currently being seen in Greece and some other eurozone countries).

Corporate bonds, however, can face more real default risks, namely that the company could go bust.

Both carry interest rate risk, which means that the price of the bond could fall substantially if interest rates rise sharply.

2.3 Equities

Again, it is impossible to consider asset classes without also looking at equities. Below is a brief description of equities. These will be more fully covered later in this workbook, in Chapter 4.

Equities, or 'shares' or 'stocks', are another major asset class.

Holding shares in a company is the same as having an ownership stake in that company. So a shareholder in, say, ABC bank is a part-owner of ABC. Income will be in the form of regular dividends paid, plus a potential capital gain if the company does well and the share price rises.

Shares in ABC are, however, riskier than bonds, for the following reasons:

- At the extreme end of the spectrum, there is always the risk that the company could go into liquidation (but, of course, in this case the holder of a bond issued by ABC may also be likely to lose out).
- More likely is the chance that the shares may go down in value, instead of up as the investor hopes.
- In addition, there is the risk that ABC will have a poor trading year: if it makes little or no profit, it may be unable to pay a dividend – or may pay a lower one than in previous years. This is a serious risk for an investor relying on dividend income.

The major reason an investor would prefer equities over bonds is the potentially greater benefits that can arise from owning shares, namely dividends, and the prospect of capital growth.

In the past, equity investments have outperformed bonds and cash over the longer term, that is a period of ten years or more, but the position today is less clear.

2.4 Property

Learning Objective

3.3.1 Know the characteristics of property investment: commercial/residential property; direct/indirect investment

3.3.2 Know the advantages and disadvantages of investing in property

Property as an asset class is unique in its distinguishing features:

- Each individual property is unique in terms of location, structure and design.
- Valuation is subjective, as property is not traded in a centralised marketplace, and continuous and reliable price data is not available.
- Property is subject to complex legal considerations and high transaction costs upon transfer.
- It is relatively illiquid as a result of not being instantly tradeable.
- It is also illiquid in another sense: the investor generally has to sell all of the property or nothing at all. It is not generally feasible for a commercial property investor to sell, for example, one factory unit out of an entire block (or at least, to do so would be commercially unattractive) – and a residential property owner cannot sell his spare bedroom to raise a little cash.
- Since property can only be purchased in discrete and sizeable units, diversification is made difficult.
- The supply of land is finite and its availability can be further restricted by legislation and local planning regulations. Therefore, price is predominantly determined by changes in demand.

Only the largest investors, generally institutional investors, can purchase sufficient properties to build a diversified portfolio. They tend to avoid residential property (although some have diversified into sizeable residential property portfolios) and instead they concentrate on commercial property, such as shops and offices, industrial property and farmland.

Some key differences between commercial and residential property are shown in the table below.

	Residential Property	Commercial Property
Direct investment	Range of investment opportunities, including second homes, holiday homes and buy-to-let	Size of investment required means direct investment in commercial property is limited to property companies and institutional investors
Tenancies	Typically short renewable leases	Long-term contracts with periods commonly in excess of ten years
Repairs	Landlord is responsible	Tenant is usually responsible
Returns	Largely linked to increase in house prices	Significant component is income return from rental income

As an asset class, property has at times provided positive real long-term returns allied to low volatility and a reliable stream of income. An exposure to property can provide diversification benefits owing to its low correlation with both traditional and alternative asset classes.

Many private investors have chosen to become involved in the property market through the buy-to-let market. Other investors wanting to include property within a diversified portfolio generally seek indirect exposure via a mutual fund, property bonds issued by insurance companies, or shares in publicly quoted property companies. It needs to be remembered, however, that investing via a mutual fund does not always mean that an investment can be readily realised. During 2008, property prices fell across the board and, as investors started to encash holdings, property funds brought in measures to stem outflows and, in some cases, imposed 12-month moratoria on encashments.

However, property can be subject to prolonged downturns, and its lack of liquidity, significant maintenance costs, high transaction costs on transfer and the risk of having commercial property with no tenant (and, therefore, no rental income) really makes only commercial property suitable as an investment for long-term investing institutions, such as pension funds. The availability of indirect investment media, however, makes property a more accessible asset class to those running smaller diversified portfolios.

3. Foreign Exchange

Learning Objective

3.4.1 Know the basic structure of the foreign exchange market including: currency quotes; settlement; spot/forward; short-term currency swaps

The foreign exchange market, which is also known as the forex market or just the FX market, refers to the trading of one currency for another. It is by far the largest market in the world.

Historically, currencies were backed by gold (as money had 'intrinsic value'). This prevented the value of money from being debased and inflation being triggered. This gold standard was replaced after the Second World War by the Bretton Woods Agreement, which aimed to prevent speculation in currency markets by fixing all currencies against the US dollar and making the dollar convertible to gold at a fixed rate of US$35 per ounce. Under this system, countries were prohibited from devaluing their currencies by more than 10%, which they might have been tempted to do to improve their trade position.

The growth of international trade, and increasing pressure for the movement of capital, eventually destabilised this agreement, and it was finally abandoned in the 1970s. Currencies were allowed to float freely against one another, leading to the development of new financial instruments and speculation in the currency markets.

Trading in currencies became 24-hour, as it could take place in the various time zones of Asia, Europe and America. London, being placed between the Asian and American time zones, was well placed to take advantage of this and has grown to become the world's largest forex market. Other large centres include the US, Japan and Singapore.

Trading of foreign currencies is always done in pairs. These are currency pairs when one currency is bought and the other is sold and the prices at which these take place make up the **exchange rate**. When the exchange rate is being quoted, the name of the currency is abbreviated to a three digit reference; so, for example, sterling is abbreviated to GBP, which you can think of as an abbreviation for Great Britain pounds.

The most commonly quoted currency pairs are:

- US dollar and the Japanese yen (USD/JPY).
- Euro and US dollar (EUR/USD).
- US dollar and Swiss franc (USD/CHF).
- British pound and US dollar (GBP/USD).

When currencies are quoted, the first currency is the base currency and the second is the counter or quote currency. The **base currency** is always equal to one unit of that currency, in other words, one pound, one dollar or one euro. For example, at the time of writing, the EUR:USD exchange rate is around 1:1.3141, which means that €1 is worth US$1.3141. When the exchange rate is going up, it means that the value of the base currency is rising relative to the other currency and is referred to as the currency strengthening, and, when the opposite is the case, the currency is said to be weakening.

When currency pairs are quoted, a market maker or foreign exchange trader will quote a **bid** and an **ask price**. Staying with the example of the EUR:USD the current quote is 1.3140/42 – the euro is not mentioned, as standard convention is that the base currency is always one unit. If you want to buy €100,000 then you will need to pay the higher of the two prices and deliver US$131,420; if you want to sell €100,000 then you get the lower of the two prices and receive US$131,400.

The forex market is an over-the-counter (OTC) market, ie, one where brokers and dealers negotiate directly with one another. The main participants are large international banks which continually provide the market with both bid (buy) and ask (sell) prices. Central banks are also major participants in foreign exchange markets, which they use to try to control money supply, inflation, and interest rates.

There are several types of transaction undertaken in the foreign exchange market, particularly:

- **Spot transactions** – the spot rate is the rate quoted by a bank for the exchange of one currency for another with immediate effect. However, it is worth noting that, in many cases, spot trades are settled – that is, the currencies actually change hands and arrive in recipients' bank accounts – two business days after the transaction date.
- **Forward transactions** – in this type of transaction, money does not actually change hands until some agreed future date. A buyer and seller agree on an exchange rate for any date in the future, for a fixed sum of money, and the transaction occurs on that date, regardless of what the market rates are then. The duration of the trade can be a few days, months or years.
- **Futures** – foreign currency futures are standardised versions of forward transactions that are traded on derivatives exchanges in standard sizes and maturity dates. The average contract length is roughly three months.
- **Swaps** – a common type of forward transaction is the currency swap. In a currency swap, two parties exchange currencies for a certain length of time and agree to reverse the transaction at a later date. These are not exchange-traded contracts and, instead, are negotiated individually between the parties to a swap. They are a type of OTC derivative (see Chapter 6).

Answers to Exercises

Exercise 1

Interest earned = €3,000 x 4% = €120

Tax deducted = 20% x €120 = €24

Amount received by Mr Evans = 80% x €120 = €96

Exercise 2

Gross rate of interest = 3%

Tax due = 20% of the gross amount

Net amount due = Gross amount (3%) less tax (3% x 20% = 0.6%) = 2.4%

Exercise 3

Interest earned = €10,000 x 3% = €300 pa and so, for six months = €150

Tax deducted = 20% x €150 = 30

Amount received by Mrs Smith = 80% x €150 = €120

End of Chapter Questions

Think of an answer for each question and refer to the appropriate section for confirmation.

1. How much net interest will be paid on a cash deposit of £10,000 deposited for six months at 2.5% pa, if the tax rate is 20%?
   Answer Reference: Section 2.1.1

2. How is the return on a Treasury bill paid?
   Answer Reference: Section 2.1.2

3. What are the advantages and disadvantages of investing in property?
   Answer Reference: Section 2.4

4. When will a spot forex trade settle?
   Answer Reference: Section 3

Chapter Four

Equities/Stocks

This syllabus area will provide approximately 9 of the 50 examination questions

1. Features and Benefits of Shares

Learning Objective

4.1.1 Know the features and benefits of ordinary and preference shares/common stock and preferred stock: dividend; capital gain; pre-emptive rights; right to vote

4.1.2 Be able to calculate the share dividend yield

In general terms, the capital of a company is made up of a combination of borrowing and the money invested by its owners. The long-term borrowing, or debt, of a company is usually referred to as bonds, and the money invested by its owners as shares, stocks or equity.

Shares are the equity capital of a company, hence the reason they are referred to as equities. They may comprise ordinary shares and preference shares.

Shares can be issued in either registered or bearer form. Holding shares in **registered** form involves the investor having their name recorded on the share register and, sometimes, being issued with a share certificate to reflect the person's ownership. However, many companies which issue registered shares now do so on a non-certificated basis, with an electronic record of ownership being sufficient.

The alternative to holding shares in registered form is to hold **bearer** shares. The person who holds, or is the bearer of, the shares is the owner. Ownership passes by transfer of the share certificate to the new owner.

1.1 Ordinary Shares and Common Stock

The share capital of a company may be made up of ordinary shares, and the ordinary shareholders own the company. If an individual were fortunate enough to own 20% of the telecoms giant Vodafone's ordinary shares, he would own one-fifth of Vodafone.

The terminology used varies from market to market, so that equity capital may be known as ordinary shares, common shares or common stock. Whatever terminology is used, they all share the same characteristics: namely, they carry the full risk and reward of investing in a company. If a company does well, its ordinary shareholders will do well.

As the ultimate owners of the company, it is the ordinary shareholders who **vote** yes or no to each resolution put forward by the company directors at company meetings. For example, an offer to take over a company may be made and the directors may propose that it is accepted but this will be subject to a vote by shareholders. If the shareholders vote no, then the directors will have to think again.

Ordinary shareholders share in the profits of the company by receiving **dividends** declared by the company, which tend to be paid half-yearly or even quarterly. The company directors will propose a dividend, and the proposed dividend will need to be ratified by the ordinary shareholders before it is formally declared as payable.

However, if the company does badly, it is also the ordinary shareholders that will suffer. If the company closes down, often described as the company being 'wound up', the ordinary shareholders are paid after everybody else. If there is nothing left, then the ordinary shareholders get nothing. If there is money left, it all belongs to the ordinary shareholders.

Some ordinary shares may be referred to as **partly paid** or **contributing** shares. This means that only part of their nominal value has been paid up. For example, if a new company was established with an initial capital of £100, this capital may be made up of 100 ordinary £1 shares. If the shareholders to whom these shares are allocated have paid £1 per share in full, then the shares are termed **fully paid**. Alternatively, the shareholders may contribute only half of the initial capital, say £50 in total, which would require a payment of 50p (£0.50) per share, that is one-half of the amount due. The shares would then be termed partly paid, but the shareholder has an obligation to pay the remaining amount when called upon to do so by the company.

1.2 Preference Shares and Preferred Stock

Some companies have preference shares or preferred stock as well as ordinary shares. The company's internal rules (its Articles of Association) set out how the preference shares differ from ordinary shares.

Preference shares are a hybrid security with elements of both debt and equity. Although they are technically a form of equity investment, they also have characteristics of debt, particularly that they pay a fixed income. Preference shares have legal priority (known as **seniority**) over ordinary shareholders in respect of earnings and, in the event of bankruptcy, in respect of assets.

Normally, preference shares:

- are non-voting, except in certain circumstances such as when their dividends have not been paid;
- pay a fixed dividend each year, the amount being set when they are first issued and which has to be paid before dividends on ordinary shares can be paid;
- rank ahead of ordinary shares in terms of being paid back if the company is wound up.

Preference shares may be cumulative, non-cumulative and/or participating.

If dividends cannot be paid in a particular year, perhaps because the company has insufficient profits, ordinary preference shares would get no dividend. However, if they were **cumulative** preference shares then the dividend entitlement accumulates. Assuming sufficient profits, the cumulative preference shares will have the arrears of dividend paid in the subsequent year. If the shares were **non-cumulative**, the dividend from the first year would be lost.

Example

If ABC shares ordinarily paid a dividend of US$2 per share, and announced that they did not have the cashflow to meet this obligation in year one, in year two, cumulative preferred shares would pay a dividend of US$4, whereas ordinary preferred shares would pay the US$2. The unpaid US$2 from the previous period would be lost.

Participating preference shares entitle the holder to a basic dividend of, say, 3% a year, but the directors can award a bigger dividend in a year when the profits exceed a certain level. In other words, the preference shareholder can participate in bumper profits.

Preference shares may also be convertible or redeemable. **Convertible** preference shares carry an option to convert into the ordinary shares of the company at set intervals and on pre-set terms.

Redeemable shares, as the name implies, have a date at which they may be redeemed; that is, the nominal value of the shares will be paid back to the preference shareholder and the shares cancelled.

4

Example

Banks and other financial institutions are regular issuers of preference shares. So, for example, an investor may have the following holding of a preference share issued by Standard Chartered – £1,000 Standard Chartered 7$^3/_8$% non-cumulative irredeemable preference shares.

This means:

- The investor will receive a fixed dividend of 7$^3/_8$% each year which is payable in two equal half-yearly instalments on 1 April and 1 November.
- The amount of the dividend is calculated by multiplying the amount of shares held (£1,000) by the interest rate of 7$^3/_8$%, which gives a total annual dividend of £73.75 gross, which will be paid in two instalments.
- The dividend will be paid providing that the company makes sufficient profits, and has to be paid before any dividend can be paid to ordinary shareholders.
- The term 'non-cumulative' means that if the company does not make sufficient profits to pay the dividend, then it is lost and the arrears are not carried forward.
- The term 'irredeemable' means that there is no fixed date for the shares to be repaid and the capital would only be repaid in the event of the company being wound up. The amount the investor would receive is the nominal value of the shares, in other words £1,000, and they would be paid out before (in preference to) the ordinary shareholders.

1.3 Benefits of Owning Shares

Holding shares in a company is having an ownership stake in that company. Ownership carries certain benefits and rights, and ordinary shareholders expect to be the major beneficiaries of a company's success. This reward or return can take one of the following forms.

1.3.1 Dividends

A dividend is the return that an investor gets for providing the risk capital for a business. Companies pay dividends out of their profits, which form part of their distributable reserves. These are the post-tax profits made over the life of a company, in excess of dividends paid.

Example

ABC plc was formed some years ago. Over the company's life it has made £20 million in profits and paid dividends of £13 million. Distributable reserves at the beginning of the year are, therefore, £7 million.

This year ABC plc makes post-tax profits of £3 million and decides to pay a dividend of £1 million. At the end of the year distributable reserves are:

	Millions
Opening balance	7
Profit after tax for year	3
	10
Dividend	(1)
Closing balance	9

Note, despite only making £3 million in the current year, it would be perfectly legal for ABC plc to pay dividends of more than £3 million because it can use the undistributed profits from previous years. This would be described as a 'naked' or 'uncovered' dividend, because the current year's profits were insufficient to fully cover the dividend. Companies occasionally do this, but it is obviously not possible to maintain this long term.

Companies seek, when possible, to pay steadily growing dividends. A fall in dividend payments can lead to a negative reaction among shareholders and a general fall in the willingness to hold the company's shares, or to provide additional capital.

Potential shareholders will compare the dividend paid on a company's shares with alternative investments. These would include other shares, bonds and bank deposits. This involves calculating the **dividend yield**.

Example

ABC plc has 20 million ordinary shares, each trading at US$2.50. It pays out a total of US$1 million in dividends. Its dividend yield is calculated by expressing the dividend as a percentage of the total value of the company's shares (the market capitalisation):

$$\frac{\text{Dividend (1m)}}{\text{Market capitalisation}} \times 100$$

So the dividend yield is:

[1m/(20m x 2.50)] x 100 = 2%

Since ABC plc paid US$1 million to shareholders of 20 million shares, the dividend yield can also be calculated on a per-share basis.

The dividend per share is 1 million/20 million shares, ie, 0.05. So 0.05/2.50 (the share price) is again 2%.

Some companies have a higher than average dividend yield, which may be because:

- The company is mature and continues to generate healthy levels of cash, but has limited growth potential, perhaps because the government regulates its selling prices, and so it distributes more of its profits rather than keeping them for reinvestment in the business. Examples are utilities, such as water or electricity companies.
- The company has a low share price for some other reason, perhaps because it is, or is expected to be, relatively unsuccessful; its comparatively high current dividend is, therefore, not expected to be sustained and its share price is not expected to rise.

In contrast, some companies might have dividend yields that are relatively low. This is generally for the following reasons:

- the share price is high, because the company is viewed by investors as having high growth prospects; or
- a large proportion of the profit being generated by the company is being ploughed back into the business, rather than being paid out as dividends.

1.3.2 Capital Gains

Capital gains can be made on shares if their prices increase over time. If an investor purchased a share for US$3, and two years later that share price has risen to US$5, then the investor has made a US$2 capital gain. If he doesn't sell the share, then the gain is described as being **unrealised**, and he runs the risk of the share price falling before he does realise the share and banks his profits.

In the recent past, the long-term total financial return from equities has been fairly evenly split between dividends and capital gain. Whereas dividends need to be reinvested in order to accumulate wealth, capital gains simply build up. However, the shares need to be sold to realise any capital gains.

1.3.3 Pre-Emptive Rights: Right to Subscribe for New Shares

If a company were able to issue new shares to anyone, then existing shareholders could lose control of the company, or at least see their share of ownership diluted. As a result, in most markets apart from the US, existing shareholders in companies are given **pre-emptive** rights to subscribe for new shares. What this means is that, unless the shareholders agree to permit the company to issue shares to others, they will be given the option to subscribe for any new share offering before it is offered to the wider public, and in many cases they receive some compensation if they decide not to do so.

Pre-emptive rights are illustrated in the following example.

Example

An investor, Mr B, holds 20,000 ordinary shares of the 100,000 issued ordinary shares in ABC plc. He therefore owns 20% of ABC plc.

If ABC plc planned to increase the number of issued ordinary shares by allowing investors to subscribe for 50,000 new ordinary shares, Mr B would be offered 20% of the new shares, ie, 10,000. This would enable Mr B to retain his 20% ownership of the enlarged company.

In summary:

Before the issue

Mr B	=	20,000	(20%)
Other shareholders	=	80,000	(80%)
Total	=	100,000	(100%)

New issue

Mr B	=	10,000
Other shareholders	=	40,000
Total	=	50,000

After the issue

Mr B	=	30,000	(20%)
Other shareholders	=	120,000	(80%)
Total	=	150,000	(100%)

A rights issue is one method by which a company can raise additional capital, complying with pre-emptive rights, with existing shareholders having the right to subscribe for new shares (see Section 3.1).

1.3.4 Right to Vote

Ordinary shareholders have the right to vote on matters presented to them at company meetings. This would include the right to vote on proposed dividends and other matters, such as the appointment, or reappointment, of directors.

The votes are normally allocated on the basis of **one share = one vote**.

The votes are cast in one of two ways:

- The individual shareholder can attend the company meeting and vote.
- The individual shareholder can appoint someone else to vote on his behalf – this is commonly referred to as **voting by proxy**.

However, some companies issue different share classes, for some of which voting rights are restricted or non-existent. This allows some shareholders to control the company while only holding a small proportion of the shares.

2. The Risks of Owning Shares

Learning Objective

4.1.3 Understand the risks associated with owning shares/stock: price risk; liquidity risk; issuer risk; foreign exchange risk

The risk(s) associated with owning shares depends on the shares held. The issuing company, including its management team, the industry it is in, and even the country or countries it operates in, contribute to determining the level of risk associated with holding any given shares. To offset this potential risk, shares offer the potential for relatively high returns when a company is successful. The main risks associated with holding shares can be classified under four headings.

2.1 Price and Market Risk

Price risk is the risk that share prices in general might fall. Even though the company involved might maintain dividend payments, investors could face a loss of capital.

Market-wide falls in equity prices occur, unfortunately, on a fairly frequent basis. For example:

- Worldwide equities fell by nearly 20% on 19 October 1987, with some shares falling by even more than this. That day is generally referred to as Black Monday, and the Dow Jones index fell by 22.3%, wiping US$500 billion off share prices. Markets across the world followed suit and collapsed in the same fashion. Central banks intervened to prevent a depression and a banking crisis and, remarkably, the markets recovered much of their losses quite quickly from the worst ever one-day crash.
- After the 1987 crash, global markets resumed the bull market trend driven by computer technology. The arrival of the internet age sparked suggestions that a new economy was in development and led to a surge in internet stocks. Many of these stocks were quoted on the NASDAQ (National Association of Securities Dealers Automated Quotations) exchange, whose index went from 600 to 5000 by the year 2000. This led the chairman of the Federal Reserve to describe investor behaviour as *'irrational exuberance'*.
- By early 2000, reality started to settle in and the 'dot.com' bubble was firmly burst, with the NASDAQ crashing to 2000. Economies went into recession and heralded a decline in world stock markets, which continued in many until 2003.
- This was followed by general increases in equity prices until falls were again seen across world stock markets in 2008 in the financial crisis.

All of this clearly demonstrates the risks associated with equity investment from general price collapses. In addition to these market-wide movements, any single company can experience dramatic falls in its share price when it discloses bad news, such as the loss of a major contract.

Price risk varies between companies: volatile shares, such as shares in investment banks, tend to exhibit more price risk than 'defensive' shares, such as utility companies and general retailers.

2.2 Liquidity Risk

Liquidity risk is the risk that shares may be difficult to sell at a reasonable price. This typically occurs in respect of shares in 'thinly traded' companies – smaller companies, or those in which there is not much trading activity. It can also happen, to a lesser degree, when share prices in general are falling, in which case the spread between the bid price (the price at which dealers will buy shares) and the offer price (the price at which dealers will sell shares) may widen.

Shares in smaller companies tend to have a greater liquidity risk than shares in larger companies – smaller companies also tend to have a wider price spread than larger, more actively traded companies.

2.3 Issuer Risk

This is the risk that the issuer collapses and the ordinary shares become worthless.

In general, it is very unlikely that larger, well-established companies would collapse, and the risk could be seen, therefore, as insignificant. Events such as the collapse of Enron and Lehman Brothers, however, show that the risk is a real and present one and cannot be ignored.

Shares in new companies, which have not yet managed to report profits, may have a substantial issuer risk.

2.4 Foreign Exchange Risk

This is the risk that currency price movements will have a negative effect on the value of an investment.

Example

For example, a European investor may buy 1,000 US shares today at, say, US$1 per share when the exchange rate is US$1:€0.75. This would give a total cost of US$1,000 or €750. Let's say that the shares rise to US$1.2 per share and the investor sells their holding for US$1,200 and so has made a gain of 20% in dollar terms. If the exchange rate changes, however, the full amount of this gain might not be realised. If the dollar has weakened to, say, US$1:€0.60, then the proceeds of sale when they are converted back into euros would only be worth €720.

Currency movements can therefore wipe out or reduce a gain, but equally can enhance a gain if the currency movement is in the opposite direction.

3. Corporate Actions

Learning Objective

4.1.4 Know the definition of a corporate action and the difference between mandatory, voluntary and mandatory with options

A corporate action occurs when a company does something that affects its share capital or its bonds. For example, most companies pay dividends to their shareholders twice a year.

Corporate actions can be classified into three types.

1. A **mandatory corporate action** is one mandated by the company, not requiring any intervention from the shareholders or bondholders. The most obvious example of a mandatory corporate action is the payment of a dividend, since all shareholders automatically receive the dividend.
2. A **mandatory corporate action with options** is an action that has some sort of default option that will occur if the shareholder does not intervene. However, until the date at which the default option occurs, the individual shareholders are given the choice to select another option. An example of a mandatory corporate action with options is a rights issue (detailed below).
3. A **voluntary corporate action** is an action that requires the shareholder to make a decision. An example is a takeover bid – if the company is being bid for, each individual shareholder will need to choose whether to accept the offer or not.

This classification is the one that is used throughout Europe and by the international central securities depositaries Euroclear and Clearstream. It should be noted that, in the US, corporate actions are simply divided into two classifications, voluntary and mandatory. The major difference between the two is therefore mandatory events with options. In the US, these types of events are split into two or more different events that have to be processed.

3.1 Types of Corporate Action

Learning Objective

4.1.5 Know the different methods of quoting securities ratios

4.1.6 Understand the following terms: bonus/scrip/capitalisation issues; rights issues/open offers; stock splits/reverse stock splits; dividend payments; takeover/merger

3.1.1 Securities Ratios

Before we look at various types of corporate action, it is necessary to know how the terms of a corporate action such as a rights issue or bonus issue are expressed – a securities ratio.

When a corporate action is announced, the terms of the event will specify what is to happen. This could be as simple as the amount of dividend that is to be paid per share. For other events, the terms will announce how many new shares the holder is entitled to receive for each existing share that they hold.

So, for example, a company may announce a bonus issue whereby it gives new shares to its investors in proportion to the shares it already holds. The terms of the bonus issue may be expressed as 1:4, which means that the investor will receive one new share for each existing four shares held. This is the standard approach used in European and Asian markets and can be simply remembered by always expressing the terms as the investor will receive 'X new shares for each Y existing shares'.

The approach differs in the US. The first number in the securities ratio indicates the final holding after the event; the second number is the original number of shares held. The above example expressed in US terms would be 5:4. So, for example, if a US company announced a 5:4 bonus issue and the investor held 10,000 shares, then the investor would end up with 12,500 shares.

3.1.2 Rights Issues

A company may wish to raise additional finance by issuing new shares. This might be to provide funds for expansion, or to repay bank loans or bond finance. In such circumstances, it is common for a company to approach its existing shareholders with a 'cash call' – they have already bought some shares in the company, so would they like to buy some more?

Company law in many countries gives a series of protections to existing shareholders. As already stated, they have pre-emptive rights – the right to buy shares so that their proportionate holding is not diluted. A rights issue can be defined as an offer of new shares to existing shareholders, pro rata to their initial holdings. Since it is an offer and the shareholders have a choice, rights issues are examples of a 'mandatory with options' type of corporate action.

As an example of a rights issue, the company might offer shareholders the right that for every four shares owned, they can buy one more at a specified price that is at a discount to the current market price.

The initial response to the announcement of a rights issue is nearly always for the share price to fall until the market has time to reflect on reasons for the rights issue and take a view on what that means for the prospects for the company. If it is to finance expansion, and the strategy makes sense to the investors, then the share price could subsequently recover. If the money is to be used for a strategy that the market does not think highly of, the response might be the opposite.

Example

ABC plc has 100 million shares in issue, currently trading at £4.00 each. To raise finance for expansion, it decides to offer its existing shareholders the right to buy one new share for every five previously held. This would be described as a one for five rights issue.

The price of the rights would be set at a discount to the prevailing market price, at, say, £3.40.

Each shareholder is given choices as to how to proceed following a rights issue. For an individual holding five shares in ABC plc, he could:

- take up the rights – by paying the £3.40 and increasing his holding in ABC plc to six shares;
- sell the rights on to another investor – the rights entitlement is transferable (often described as **renounceable**) and will have a value because it enables the purchase of a share at the discounted price of £3.40;
- do nothing – if the investor chooses this option, the company's advisers will sell the rights at the best available price and pass on the proceeds (after charges) to the shareholder.

Alternatively, an investor holding, say, 5,000 shares would have the right to buy 1,000. He could sell sufficient of the rights to raise cash and use this cash to take up the rest.

The share price of the investor's existing shares will also adjust to reflect the additional shares that are being issued. So, if the investor originally had five shares priced at £4 each, worth £20, and can acquire one new share at £3.40, on taking up the rights the investor will have six shares worth £23.40 or £3.90 each. The share price will therefore change to reflect the effect of the rights issue.

The company and its investment banking advisers will have to consider the numbers carefully. If the price at which new shares are offered is too high, the cash call might flop. This would be embarrassing, and potentially costly for any institution that has **underwritten** the issue. Underwriters of a share issue agree, for a fee, to buy any portion of the issue not taken up in the market at the issue price. The underwriters then sell the shares they have bought when market conditions seem opportune to them, and may make a gain or a loss on this sale. The underwriters agree to buy the shares if no one else will, and the company's investment bank will probably underwrite some of the issue itself.

3.1.3 Open Offers

In many European, Middle Eastern and Far East markets, a variation on the rights issue theme is sometimes used when a company wants to raise finance: an open offer.

An open offer is made to existing shareholders and gives the holders the opportunity to subscribe for additional shares in the company or for other securities, normally in proportion to their holdings. In this way it is similar to a rights issue, but the difference is that the right to buy the offered securities is not transferable and so cannot be sold.

For normal open offers, holders of the shares cannot apply for more than their entitlement. However, an open offer can be structured so that holders may be allowed to apply for more than their pro rata entitlement, with the possibility of being scaled back in the event of the offer being oversubscribed.

3.1.4 Bonus Issues

A bonus issue (also known as a **scrip** or **capitalisation** issue) is a corporate action when the company gives existing shareholders extra shares without them having to subscribe any further funds.

The company is simply increasing the number of shares held by each shareholder, and capitalises earnings by transfer to shareholders' funds. It is a mandatory corporate action.

Example

XYZ plc's shares currently trade at £12 each.

The company decides to make a one for one bonus issue, giving each shareholder an additional share for each share they currently hold.

The result is that a single shareholder that held one share worth £12 now has two shares worth the same amount in total. As the number of shares in issue has doubled, the share price halves to £6 each.

The reason for making a bonus issue is to increase the liquidity of the company's shares in the market and to bring about a lower share price. The logic is that if a company's share price becomes too high, it may be unattractive to investors.

3.1.5 Stock Splits and Reverse Stock Splits

An alternative to a bonus issue as a way of reducing a share price is to have a subdivision or stock split whereby each share is split into a number of shares.

For example, a company with shares having a nominal value of €5 each and a market price of €10 may have a split whereby each share is divided into five shares, each with a nominal value of €1. In theory, the market price of each new share should be €2 (€10 ÷ 5).

It might appear as though there is little difference between a bonus issue and a stock split, but a bonus issue does not alter the nominal value of the company's shares.

A reverse split or consolidation is the opposite of a split: shares are combined or consolidated. For example, a company with a share price of €0.10 may consolidate ten shares into one. The market price of each new share should then be €1 (€0.10 x 10). A company may do this if the share price has fallen to a low level and they wish to make their shares more marketable.

3.1.6 Dividends

Dividends are an example of a mandatory corporate action and represent the part of a company's profit that is passed to its shareholders.

Dividends for many large companies are paid twice a year, with the first dividend being declared by the directors and paid approximately halfway through the year (commonly referred to as the interim dividend). The second dividend is paid after approval by shareholders at the company's annual general meeting (AGM), held after the end of the company's financial year, and is referred to as the final dividend for the year.

The amount paid per share may vary, as it depends on factors such as the overall profitability of the company and any plans it might have for future expansion.

The individual shareholders will receive the dividends either by cheque or by the money being transferred straight into their bank accounts.

A practical difficulty, especially in a large company where shares change hands frequently, is determining who is the correct person to receive dividends. There are, therefore, procedures to minimise the extent that people receive dividends they are not entitled to, or fail to receive the dividend to which they are entitled.

Shares are bought and sold with the right to receive the next declared dividend up to the date when the declaration is actually made. Up to that point the shares are described as **cum-dividend**. If the shares are purchased cum-dividend, the purchaser will receive the declared dividend. For the period between declaration and the dividend payment date, the shares go **ex-dividend**. Buyers of shares when they are ex-dividend are not entitled to the declared dividend.

From October 2014, the standard settlement period across Europe is to change to T+2. This means that a trade will be settled two business days after it is executed so, for example, a trade executed on Monday would settle on the following Wednesday. As a result, the dividend timetable is also changing, as the following example illustrates.

Example

The sequence of events for a company listed on the London Stock Exchange (LSE) might be as follows:

ABC plc calculates its interim profits (for the six months to 30 June) and decides to pay a dividend of £0.08 per share. It announces ('declares') the dividend in August and states that it will be due to those shareholders who are entered on the shareholders' register on Friday 9 October. The payment of the dividend will then be made to those shareholders at a later specified date.

The 9 October date, is variously known as the:

- record date;
- register date; or
- books closed date.

Given the record date of Friday 9 October, the LSE sets the ex-dividend date as Thursday 8 October.

From October 2014, the ex-dividend date is invariably a Thursday so that all market participants know when it will take place and, on this day, the shares will go ex-dividend and should fall in price by £0.08. This is because new buyers of ABC plc's shares will not be entitled to the dividend.

Problems can occur – if an investor bought shares in ABC plc on 7 October and, for some reason, the trade did not settle on Friday 9 October, they would not receive the dividend. A dividend claim would be made and the buyer's broker would then recover the money via the seller's broker.

3.1.7 Takeovers and Mergers

Companies seeking to expand can grow organically or by buying other companies. In a takeover, which may be friendly or hostile, one company (the predator) seeks to acquire another company (the target).

In a successful takeover, the predator company will buy more than 50% of the shares of the target company. When the predator holds more than half of the shares of the target company, the predator is described as having gained control of the target company. Usually, the predator company will look to buy all of the shares in the target company, perhaps for cash, but usually using its own shares, or a mixture of cash and shares.

A merger is a similar transaction when the two companies are of similar size and agree to merge their interests. However, in a merger it is usual for one company to exchange new shares for the shares of the other. As a result, the two companies effectively merge to form a bigger entity.

3.2 Company Meetings

Learning Objective

4.1.7 Know the purpose and format of annual company meetings

Public companies must hold annual general meetings (AGMs) at which shareholders are given the opportunity to question the directors about the company's strategy and operations. The name for these meetings varies from country to country, so in some it is just a general meeting, in others a general assembly and in the US, simply a stockholders' meeting.

The shareholders are also given the opportunity to vote on matters such as the appointment and removal of directors and the payment of the final dividend recommended by the directors.

Most matters put to the shareholders are **ordinary resolutions**, requiring a simple majority (more than 50%) of those shareholders voting to be passed.

Matters of major importance, such as a proposed change to the company's constitution, require a **special resolution** which will require a larger number of shareholders to vote in favour, generally at least 75% of those voting.

Shareholders can either vote in person or have their vote registered at the meeting by completing a proxy voting form, enabling someone else to register their vote on their behalf.

4. Primary and Secondary Markets

Learning Objective

4.1.8 Know the differences between the primary market and secondary market

When a company decides to seek a listing for its shares, the process is described in a number of ways:

- becoming **listed** or **quoted**;
- **floating** on the stock market;
- **going public**; or
- making an **initial public offering (IPO)**.

Other relevant terminology is 'primary market' and 'secondary market'. The term **primary market** refers to the marketing of new shares in a company to investors for the first time. Once they have acquired shares, the investors may at some point wish to dispose of some or all of their shares and will generally do this through a stock exchange.

This latter process is referred to as 'dealing on the **secondary market**'.

Primary markets exist to raise capital and enable surplus funds to be matched with investment opportunities, while secondary markets allow the primary market to function efficiently by facilitating two-way trade in issued securities.

A stock exchange is an organised marketplace for issuing and trading securities by members of that exchange. Each exchange has its own rules and regulations for companies seeking a listing, and continuing obligations for those already listed. All stock exchanges provide both a primary and a secondary market.

5. Depositary Receipts

Learning Objective

4.1.9 Understand the characteristics of depositary receipts: American depositary receipt; global depositary receipt; dividend payments; how created/pre-release facility; rights

American depositary receipts (ADRs) were introduced in 1927 and were originally designed to enable US investors to hold overseas shares without the high dealing costs and settlement delays associated with overseas equity transactions.

An ADR is dollar-denominated and issued in bearer form, with a depository bank as the registered shareholder. They confer the same shareholder rights as if the shares had been purchased directly.

The depository bank makes arrangements for issues such as the payment of dividends, also denominated in US dollars, and voting via a proxy at shareholder meetings. The beneficial owner of the underlying shares may cancel the ADR at any time and become the registered owner of the shares.

The US is a huge pool of potential investment, and so ADRs enable non-US companies to attract US investors to raise funds. ADRs are listed and freely traded on the NYSE (New York Stock Exchange) and NASDAQ. An ADR market also exists on the LSE.

Each ADR has a particular number of underlying shares, or is represented by a fraction of an underlying share. For example, Volkswagen AG (the motor vehicle manufacturer) is listed in Frankfurt and has two classes of shares listed – ordinary shares and preference shares. There are separate ADRs in existence for the ordinary shares and preference shares. Each ADR represents 0.2 individual Volkswagen shares. ADRs give investors a simple, reliable and cost-efficient way to invest in other markets and avoid high dealing and settlement costs. Other well-known companies, such as BP, Nokia, Royal Dutch and Vodafone, have issued ADRs.

ADRs are not the only type of depositary receipts that may be issued. Those issued outside the US are termed global depositary receipts (GDRs). These have been issued since 1990 and are traded on many exchanges. Increasingly, depositary receipts are issued by Asian and emerging market issuers.

For example, more than 400 GDRs from 37 countries are quoted and traded on a section of the LSE and are settled in US dollars through Euroclear or the DTCC (Depository Trust & Clearing Corporation) Depository Bank.

Both Euroclear and DTCC will collect the dividend on the underlying share and then convert this into payments that can be paid out to the GDR holders. Any voting rights are exercised through the Depository Bank, but GDR holders are not able to take up rights issues and instead these are sold and the cash distributed.

Up to 20% of a company's voting share capital may be converted into depositary receipts. In certain circumstances, the custodian bank may issue depositary receipts before the actual deposit of the underlying shares. This is called a **pre-release** of the ADR and so trading may take place in this pre-release form. A pre-release is closed out as soon as the underlying shares are delivered by the depository bank.

6. World Stock Markets

Learning Objective

4.1.10 Know the role of stock markets

4.1.12 Know how shares are traded: on-exchange/off-exchange; multilateral trading facilities; order-driven/quote-driven

A stock exchange is an organised marketplace for the issuing and trading of securities by members of that exchange. Stock exchanges have been around for hundreds of years and can be found in major cities across the world.

Companies with stocks traded on an exchange are said to be **listed**, and they must meet specific criteria, which vary across exchanges. Each exchange has its own rules and regulations for companies seeking a listing, and continuing obligations for those already listed.

Most stock exchanges began as physical meeting places, each with a **trading floor** where traders made deals face-to-face in an **open outcry** marketplace; however, most exchanges are now electronic, or at least partially electronic, as is the case with the NYSE. Trading is conducted through trading systems broadly categorised as either quote-driven or order-driven.

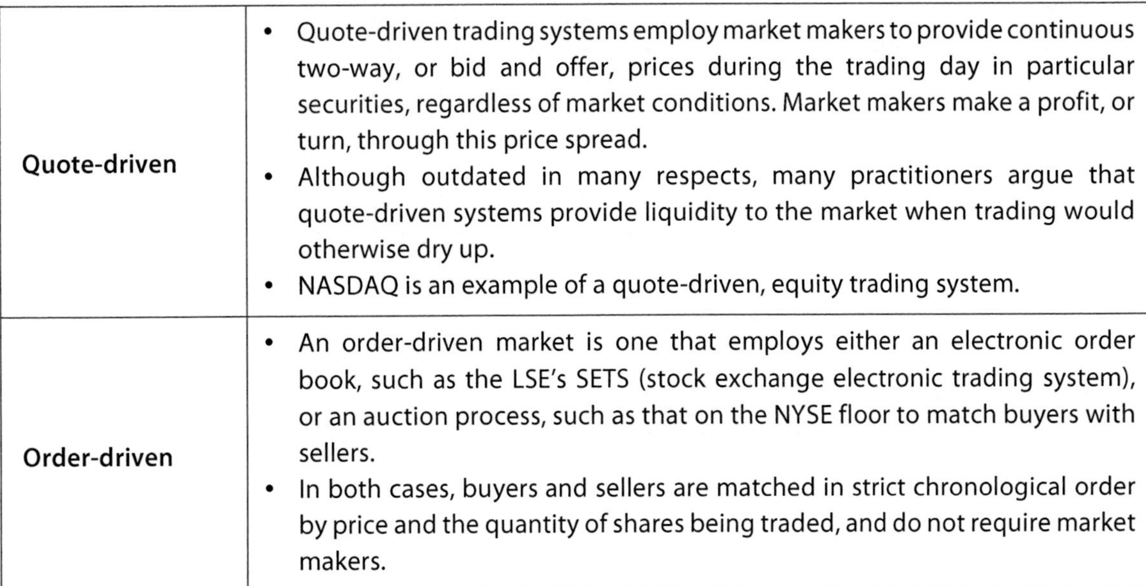

Quote-driven	• Quote-driven trading systems employ market makers to provide continuous two-way, or bid and offer, prices during the trading day in particular securities, regardless of market conditions. Market makers make a profit, or turn, through this price spread. • Although outdated in many respects, many practitioners argue that quote-driven systems provide liquidity to the market when trading would otherwise dry up. • NASDAQ is an example of a quote-driven, equity trading system.
Order-driven	• An order-driven market is one that employs either an electronic order book, such as the LSE's SETS (stock exchange electronic trading system), or an auction process, such as that on the NYSE floor to match buyers with sellers. • In both cases, buyers and sellers are matched in strict chronological order by price and the quantity of shares being traded, and do not require market makers.

Most stock exchanges operate order-driven systems, how they operate can be seen by looking at the following:

- In order-driven systems, stock exchange member firms (investment banks and brokers) input orders via computer terminals. These orders may be for the member firms themselves, or for their clients.
- Very simply, the way the system operates is that these orders will be added to the buy queue or the sell queue, or executed immediately. Investors who add their order to the relevant queue are prepared to hold out for the price they want.
- Those seeking immediate execution will trade against the queue of buyers (if they are selling) or against the sellers' queue (if they are buying).

For a liquid stock, there will be a deep order book – the term 'deep' implies that there are lots of orders waiting to be dealt on either side. The top of the queues might look like this:

Buy Queue		**Sell Queue**	
We will buy for at most		We will sell for at least	
7,000 shares	1.24	3,500 shares	1.25
5,150 shares	1.23	1,984 shares (2)	1.26
19,250 shares (1)	1.22	75,397 shares (2)	1.26
44,000 shares (1)	1.22	17,300 shares	1.27

Queue priority is given on the basis of price and then time. So, for the equally priced orders noted (1), the order to buy 19,250 shares must have been placed before the 44,000 order – hence its position higher up the queue. Similarly, for the orders noted (2), the order to sell 1,984 shares must have been input before the order to sell 75,397 shares.

As an alternative to trading on a stock exchange in the US and Europe, trades can be conducted through multilateral trading facilities (MTFs) which have emerged as powerful competitors to traditional exchanges. Examples of MTFs include BATS Europe and CHI-X Europe.

As well as trading on a stock exchange or multilateral trading facility, trades can also be executed away from the exchange directly between market counterparties. This is known as 'off-exchange' trading and is used, for example, where the size of the order from an institutional investor is too large to be executed on-exchange and the deal has to be negotiated with other potential investors.

7. Stock Market Indices

Learning Objective

4.1.11 Know the types and uses of a stock exchange index

As well as providing information on how markets are performing, stock market indices are a useful tool for investors, as they provide a realistic benchmark against which the performance of a portfolio can be judged.

Stock market indices were originally designed to provide an impressionistic mood of the market and, as such, were not constructed in a particularly scientific manner. In recent years, however, index construction has become more of a science, as performance measurement has come under increased scrutiny and the growth of index-related products has necessitated the need for more representative measures of market movements, with greater transparency surrounding their construction.

Most stock market indices have the following four uses:

- To act as a market barometer. Most equity indices provide a comprehensive record of historic price movements, thereby facilitating the assessment of trends. Plotted graphically, these price movements may be of particular interest to technical analysts and momentum investors by assisting in identifying the right point to buy or sell securities, an approach referred to as 'market timing'.
- To assist in performance measurement. Most equity indices can be used as performance benchmarks against which portfolio performance can be judged.
- To act as the basis for index tracker funds, exchange-traded funds (ETFs), index derivatives and other index-related products.
- To support portfolio management research and asset allocation decisions.

As well as considering which market they are tracking, it is important to also understand how the index has been calculated. Early indices, such as the Dow Jones Industrial Average (DJIA), are price-weighted so that it is only the price of each stock within the index that is considered when calculating the index. This means that no account is taken of the relative size of a company contained within an index, and the share price movement of one can have a disproportionate effect on the index.

Following on from these earlier indices, broader-based indices were calculated based on a greater range of shares, and which also took into account the relative market capitalisation of each stock in the index to give a more accurate indication of how the market was moving. This development process is ongoing, and most market capitalisation-weighted indices have a further refinement in that they now take account of the free-float capitalisation of their constituents. This float-adjusted calculation aims to exclude shareholdings held by large investors and governments that are not readily available for trading.

There are now over 3,000 equity indices worldwide, some of which track the fortunes of a single market while others cover a particular region, sector or a range of markets. Some of the main indices that are regularly quoted in the financial press are shown below.

Country	Name
US	DJIA: providing a narrow view of the US stock market (30 stocks)
	S&P 500 (Standard & Poor's): providing a wider view of the US stock market
	NASDAQ Composite: focusing on the shares traded on NASDAQ, including many technology companies
UK	FTSE (Financial Times Stock Exchange) 100: this is an index of the largest 100 UK companies, commonly referred to as the Footsie. The Footsie covers about 80% of the UK market by value
	FTSE All Share: this index covers over 600 companies (including the FTSE 350) and accounts for about 98% of the UK market by value. It is often used as the benchmark against which diversified share portfolios are assessed
Japan	NIKKEI 225
France	CAC 40
Germany	Xetra DAX
India	BSE Sensex
China	SSE Composite
Singapore	Straits Times Index
Australia	S&P/ASX200

8. Settlement Systems

Learning Objective

4.1.13 Understand how settlement takes place: process; settlement cycles

Settlement is the final phase of the trading process, and the generally accepted method is **delivery versus payment (DVP)**, which requires the simultaneous exchange of stock and cash.

Electronic systems are used to achieve this by a process known as **book entry transfer**, which involves changing electronic records of ownership rather than issuing new share certificates. Share certificates are instead either **immobilised** in a vault or, more usually, they are **dematerialised**, which means that paper share certificates are dispensed with altogether.

The exact process used for settlement will vary from country to country, but the following diagram illustrates the general principles of how a sale of shares between two counterparties on a recognised exchange is input, matched and settled.

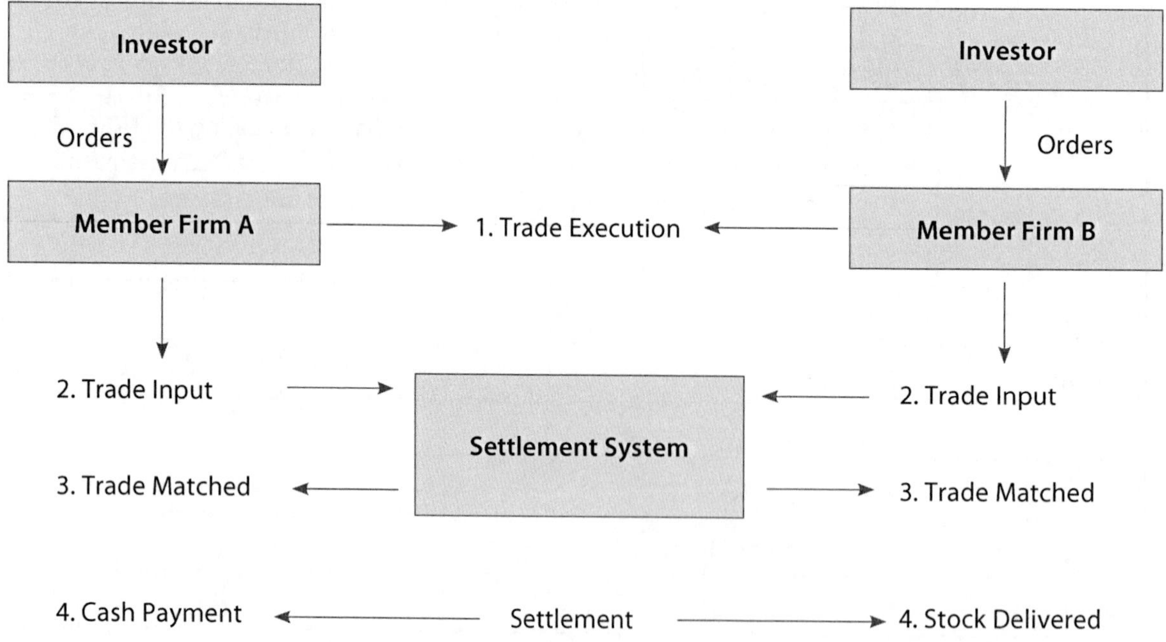

1. Investors place their orders with a broker who is a member of the stock exchange and who will then execute the trade using the exchange's trading system.
2. Once the trade is executed, details of the trade are input to the settlement system by the broker or sent automatically from the trading system.
3. The settlement system checks that the two sets of instruction agree and, when that is the case, the trade is matched and ready for settlement on the intended settlement day.
4. On settlement day, the seller's account is credited with the proceeds of sale and the securities are delivered to the buyer.

Settlement takes place once the trade instructions are matched and the intended settlement date is reached, provided that the seller has the stock to deliver and the buyer has the necessary cash. The intended settlement date will follow a settlement cycle that is standardised for each market. For example, European equity trades are settled at T+2 which means that the trade will settle two business days after the trade date – so, a trade executed on Monday should settle two business days later on Wednesday.

End of Chapter Questions

Think of an answer for each question and refer to the appropriate section for confirmation.

1. What are the features of a cumulative preference share?
   Answer Reference: Section 1.2

2. Why might a company have a higher than average dividend yield?
   Answer Reference: Section 1.3.1

3. When a shareholder appoints someone to vote on his behalf at a company meeting, what is it referred to as?
   Answer Reference: Sections 1.3.4 & 3.2

4. What options are available to an investor in a rights issue?
   Answer Reference: Section 3.1.2

5. Under what type of corporate action would an investor receive additional shares without making any payment?
   Answer Reference: Section 3.1.4

6. What is the key characteristic of an order-driven trading system?
   Answer Reference: Section 6

7. What is the name of the trading system used in Germany?
   Answer Reference: Section 7

8. What is the function of a stock market index?
   Answer Reference: Section 7

9. The CAC 40 index relates to which market?
   Answer Reference: Section 7

10. What is the meaning of DvP?
    Answer Reference: Section 8

Chapter Five

Bonds

This syllabus area will provide approximately 5 of the 50 examination questions

1. Introduction

Although bonds do not often generate as much media attention as shares, they are the larger market of the two in terms of global investment value. As we saw in Chapter 1, the value of outstanding debt globally totalled close to US$100 trillion in 2013 compared to an equity market capitalisation of US$64 trillion at the same time.

Bonds are roughly equally split between government and corporate bonds. Government bonds are issued by national governments and by supranational agencies such as the European Investment Bank and the World Bank. Corporate bonds are issued by companies, such as large banks and other large corporate listed companies.

2. Characteristics of Bonds

2.1 Definition of a Bond

Learning Objective

5.1.1 Understand the characteristics and terminology of bonds: coupon; redemption; nominal value

A bond is, very simply, a loan.

A company or government that needs to raise money to finance an investment could borrow money from its bank or, alternatively, it could issue a bond to raise the funds it needs by borrowing from the investing public.

With a bond, an investor lends in return for the promise to have the loan repaid on a fixed date and (usually) a series of interest payments.

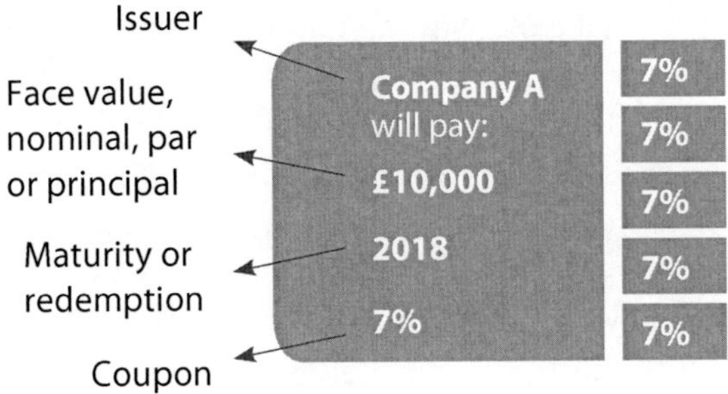

Bonds are commonly referred to as loan stock, debt and (in the case of those which pay fixed income) fixed-interest securities.

The feature that distinguishes a bond from most loans is that a bond is tradeable. Investors can buy and sell bonds without the need to refer to the original borrower.

Although there is a wide variety of fixed interest securities in issue, they all share similar characteristics. These can be described by looking at an example of a US government bond.

Nominal[1]	US$10,000
Stock[2]	Treasury bond
Coupon[3]	7.5%
Redemption date[4]	2024
Price[5]	US$146.80
Value[6]	US$14,680

Let's assume that an investor has purchased a holding of US$10,000 7.5% Treasury bond 2024 as shown in the table above.

Each of the terms in the table are explained here:

1. **Nominal** – this is the amount of stock purchased and should not be confused with the amount invested or the cost of purchase. This is the amount on which interest will be paid and the amount that will eventually be repaid. It is also known as the 'par' or 'face' value of the bond.
2. **Stock** – the name given to identify the stock and the borrower, which in this case is the US government. As will be seen later, the term 'Treasury bond' represents US government bonds issued with relatively long periods to maturity. However, the term is also used to describe bonds issued by many other countries.
3. **Coupon** – this is the amount of interest rate paid per year, expressed as a percentage of the face value of the bond. The bond issuer will pay the coupon to the bondholder. The rate is quoted gross and will normally be paid in two separate and equal half-yearly interest payments. The annual amount of interest paid is calculated by multiplying the nominal amount of stock held by the coupon; that is, in this case, US$10,000 times 7.5%.
4. **Redemption date** – this is the date at which the issue expires, and the lender will repay the borrower the sum borrowed. Repayment of principal will take place at the same time that the final interest payment is made. The amount repaid will be the nominal amount of stock held which, in this case, is US$10,000. Redemption date is also known as the 'maturity date'.
5. **Price** – this stock can be freely traded at any time on the New York Stock Exchange (NYSE) and, as mentioned above, it is quoted at US$146.80. The convention in the bond markets is to quote stock per US$100 nominal of stock. In this example, the price quoted is US$146.80 and so each US$100 nominal of stock purchased will cost US$146.80 before any brokerage costs.
6. **Value** – the value of the stock is calculated by multiplying the nominal amount of stock by the current price. Comparing the nominal value of the stock of US$10,000 to the current market value of US$14,680 (US$10,000 ÷ US$100 x US$146.80) – in other words, ignoring the coupon – the investor will make a loss of US$4,680 if the stock is held until redemption.

2.2 Advantages, Disadvantages and Risks of Investing in Bonds

Learning Objective

5.1.3 Know the advantages and disadvantages of investing in government bonds

5.2.3 Know the advantages and disadvantages of investing in corporate bonds

As one of the main asset classes, bonds clearly have a role to play in most portfolios.

2.2.1 Advantages

Their main advantages are:

- for fixed interest bonds, a regular and certain flow of income;
- for most bonds, a fixed maturity date (but there are bonds which have no redemption date, and others which may be repaid on either of two dates or between two dates – some at the investor's option and some at the issuer's option);
- a range of income yields to suit different investment and tax situations;
- relative security of capital for more highly rated bonds.

2.2.2 Disadvantages

Their main disadvantages are:

- the real value of the income flow is eroded by the effects of inflation (except in the case of index-linked bonds);
- bonds carry elements of risk; see Section 2.2.3.

2.2.3 Risks

There are a number of risks attached to holding bonds, some of which have already been considered.

Bonds generally have **default risk** (the issuer might be a company that could go out of business and/or will not repay the capital at the maturity date) and **price risk**.

It used to be said that most government bonds had only price risk as there was little or no risk that the government would fail to pay the interest or repay the capital on the bonds.

Recent turmoil in government bond markets, however, resulted from fears that certain European governments might be unable to meet their obligations on these loans, and the prices of their bonds fell significantly as a result.

Price (or market) risk is of particular concern to bondholders who are open to the effect of movements in general interest rates, which can have a significant impact on the value of their holdings.

This is best explained by two simple examples.

Example

Interest rates are approximately 5%, and the government issues a bond with a coupon rate of 5% interest. Three months later interest rates have doubled to 10%.

What will happen to the value of the bond?

The value of the bond will fall substantially. Its 5% interest is no longer attractive, so its resale price will fall to compensate, and to make the return it offers more competitive.

Example

Interest rates are approximately 5%, and the government issues a bond with a coupon rate of 5% interest. Interest rates generally fall to 2.5%.

What will happen to the value of the bond?

The value of the bond will rise substantially. Its 5% interest is very attractive, so its resale price will rise to compensate, and make the return it offers fall to more realistic levels.

As the above examples illustrate, there is an inverse relationship between interest rates and bond prices:

- If interest rates increase, bond prices will decrease.
- If interest rates decrease, bond prices will increase.

As long as the interest being paid on the government bond is near to the interest rate available on the market, there is little risk that the resale value will be significantly different from the purchase price. In other words, the government bond has price risk or market risk only when the coupon rate of interest differs markedly from market rates.

Detailed below are some of the other main types of risk associated with holding bonds.

- **Early redemption** – the risk that the issuer may invoke a call provision and redeem the bond early (if the bond is callable).
- **Seniority risk** – this relates to the seniority with which corporate debt is ranked in the event of the issuer's liquidation. If the company raises more borrowing and it is entitled to be repaid before the existing bonds, then the bonds have suffered from seniority risk.
- **Inflation risk** – the risk of inflation rising unexpectedly and eroding the real value of the bond's coupon and redemption payment.
- **Liquidity risk** – liquidity is the ease with which a security can be converted into cash. Some bonds are more easily sold at a fair market price than others.
- **Exchange rate risk** – bonds denominated in a currency different from that of the investor's home currency are potentially subject to adverse exchange rate movements.

2.3 Credit Rating Agencies

Learning Objective

5.2.4 Understand the role of credit rating agencies and the difference between investment and non-investment grades

The credit risk, or probability of an issuer defaulting on their payment obligations, and the extent of the resulting loss, can be assessed by reference to the independent credit ratings given to most bond issues.

There are more than 70 agencies throughout the world, and preferred agencies vary from country to country. The three most prominent credit rating agencies are:

- Standard & Poor's (S&P);
- Moody's; and
- Fitch Ratings.

The table below shows the credit ratings available from the three companies.

Bond Credit Ratings

Credit Risk		Moody's	Standard & Poor's	Fitch Ratings
Investment Grade				
Highest quality		Aaa	AAA	AAA
High quality	Very strong	Aa	AA	AA
Upper medium grade	Strong	A	A	A
Medium grade		Baa	BBB	BBB
Non-Investment Grade				
Lower medium grade	Somewhat speculative	Ba	BB	BB
Low grade	Speculative	B	B	B
Poor quality	May default	Caa	CCC	CCC
Most speculative		C	CC	CC
No interest being paid or bankruptcy petition filed		C	D	C
In default		C	D	D

Standard & Poor's and Fitch Ratings refine their ratings by adding a plus or minus sign to show relative standing within a category, while Moody's does the same by the addition of a 1, 2 or 3.

As can be seen, bond issues, subject to credit ratings, can be divided into two distinct categories: those accorded an investment grade rating, and those categorised as non-investment grade, or speculative. The latter are also known as 'high-yield' or – for the worst-rated – 'junk' bonds. Investment grade issues offer the greatest liquidity and certainty of repayment. Note that these terms are not actually used by the agencies but inferred by industry practice.

Very few organisations, with the exception of supranational agencies and some western governments, are awarded a triple-A rating, though the bond issues of most large corporations boast a credit rating within the investment grade categories.

3. Government Bonds

Learning Objective

5.1.2 Know the definition and features of government bonds: US; UK; France; Germany; Japan

Governments issue bonds to finance their spending and investment plans and to bridge the gap between their actual spending and the tax and other forms of income that they receive. Issuance of bonds is high when tax revenues are significantly lower than government spending.

Western governments are major borrowers of money, so the volume of government bonds in issue is very large and forms a major part of the investment portfolio of many institutional investors (such as pension funds and insurance companies).

The following section is a brief review of the characteristics of selected government bond markets for the most widely traded government bonds.

3.1 United States

The US government bond market is the largest and most liquid in the world. Government bonds issued by the US government are generally known as Treasuries and there are four main marketable types, namely: Treasury bills, Treasury notes, Treasury bonds and Treasury inflation-protected securities.

- **Treasury bills** – a money market instrument used to finance the government's short-term borrowing needs. They have maturities of less than a year and are typically issued with maturities of 28 days, 91 days and 182 days. They are zero coupon instruments that pay no interest and instead are issued at a discount to their maturity value. Once issued, they trade in the secondary market and are priced on a yield-to-maturity basis.
- **Treasury notes** – conventional government bonds that have a fixed coupon and redemption date. They have maturity dates ranging from more than one year, to not more than ten years from their issue date. They are commonly issued with maturities of two, five and ten years.
- **Treasury bonds** – again conventional government bonds, but with maturities of more than ten years from their issue date, most commonly issued with maturities of 30 years.

- **Treasury inflation-protected securities** – these are index-linked bonds and are referred to as TIPS. The principal value of the bond is adjusted regularly, based on movements in the consumer price index (CPI) to account for the impact of inflation. Interest payments are paid half-yearly and, unlike the UK version, the coupon remains constant but is paid on the changing principal value.

STRIPS (separate trading of registered interest and principal securities) are also traded based on the stripped elements of Treasury notes, bonds and TIPS. Each bond is broken down into its underlying cash flows – that is, each individual interest payment plus the single redemption payment. Each is then traded as a separate zero coupon bond (ZCB).

US Treasuries are traded for settlement the next day. They have been issued in book entry form since 1986 – that is, entry on the bond register and transfers can only take place electronically and no physical bond certificates are issued. Interest is paid on a semi-annual basis.

In addition to government bonds, federal agencies and municipal authorities also issue bonds. Some of the biggest issuers of bonds are Fannie Mae and Freddie Mac, which issue bonds to support house purchase activity.

Municipal bonds are issued by states, cities, counties and other government entities to raise money to build schools, highways, hospitals and sewer systems, as well as many other projects. Interest is usually paid semi-annually, and many are exempt from both federal and state taxes.

3.2 United Kingdom

UK government bonds are known as **gilts**. When physical certificates were issued, historically they used to have a gold or gilt edge to them, hence they are known as 'gilts' or 'gilt-edged stock'. The bonds are issued on behalf of the government by the Debt Management Office (DMO).

Conventional government bonds are instruments that carry a fixed coupon and a single repayment date, such as 5% Treasury Gilt 2018. This type of bond represents the majority of government bonds in issue.

The other main type of bond issued by the UK government is index-linked bonds. Index-linked bonds are bonds where the coupon and the redemption amount are increased by the amount of inflation over the life of the bond; they are similar to the US TIPS.

As well as categorising government bonds by type, another common division is by how many years remain until redemption. UK government stocks are classified into the following:

- zero–seven years remaining: short-dated.
- Seven–15 years remaining: medium-dated.
- 15 years and over remaining: long-dated.

In 2005, the DMO issued new gilts with redemption dates 50 years later for the first time. Although these are classified within the banding of 15 years and over, they are often referred to as 'ultra-long' gilts.

Gilts are traded for settlement the next day. Settlement takes place electronically and transfers take place by book entry. Interest is paid on a semi-annual basis.

3.3 Germany

The main types of German government bonds are **Bunds**, **Schatz** and **Bobls**. Bunds are longer-term instruments; Schatz are issued with two-year maturities; Bobls are issued with five-year maturities.

Bunds are issued with maturities of between eight and 30 years, but the most common maturity is ten years. The Bund market is large and liquid and the yield on Bunds sets the benchmark for other European government bonds.

Domestic trades settle two business days after trade date. Settlement of international trades follows the practice in the eurobond market and is for T+2 settlement, that is two business days later. All settlement takes place electronically by book entry. Interest on Bunds is paid on an annual basis.

3.4 France

French government debt is made up of longer-term instruments known as **OATS** and shorter-dated stocks known as **BTANs**, which have maturities up to five years.

Trading in OATS in both the domestic and international market is for T+2, that is two business days later. Trading in BTANs, however, is for T+1 in domestic markets and T+2 for international settlement. All settlement takes place electronically by book entry.

Interest on OATS is paid on an annual basis.

3.5 Japan

The Japanese government bond market is one of the largest in the world and its bonds are usually referred to as JGBs.

JGBs are classified into six categories:

- short-term bonds;
- medium-term bonds;
- long-term bonds;
- super-long-term bonds;
- individual investor bonds;
- inflation-indexed bonds.

Short-term JGBs have maturities of six months and one year and are issued as ZCBs; in other words they are issued at a discount, carry no interest and are repaid at their face value.

Medium, long and super-long JGBs are conventional bonds and so have fixed coupons that are paid semi-annually and have set redemption dates. The individual investor bonds and 15-year super-long JGBs pay floating interest rates.

Inflation-indexed bonds operate in a similar way to TIPS, that is, the principal amount is inflation-adjusted, based on movements in the CPI, and the coupon is fixed but payable on the inflation-adjusted principal amount.

Not all bonds are listed, and most trading takes place in the over-the-counter (OTC) market. Settlement varies depending upon the type of trade, but is typically T+3. Stock traded on the Tokyo Stock Exchange settles three days after trade date.

3.6 Primary Market Issuance

Government bonds are usually issued through agencies that are part of that country's Treasury department.

Example

In the UK, when a new gilt is issued, the process is handled by the DMO, which is the agency acting on behalf of the Treasury.

Issues are typically made in the form of an auction, where large investors (such as banks, pension funds and insurance companies) submit competitive bids. Often they will each bid for several million pounds' worth of an issue.

Issue amounts are normally between £0.5 billion and £2 billion. The DMO accepts bids from those prepared to pay the highest price.

Smaller investors are able to submit non-competitive bids. Advertisements in the *Financial Times* and other newspapers will include details of the offer and an application form.

Non-competitive bids can be submitted for up to £500,000, and the applicant will pay the average of the prices paid by competitive bidders.

The issuers for the government bonds described above are as follows:

- **US**: Bureau of the Fiscal Service.
- **UK**: Debt Management Office.
- **Germany**: Finanzagentur GmbH.
- **France**: Agence France Trésor.
- **Japan**: Ministry of Finance.

4. Corporate Bonds

Learning Objective

5.2.1 Know the definitions and features of the following types of bond: zero coupon; convertible

A corporate bond is a bond that is issued by a company, as the name suggests.

The term is usually applied to longer-term debt instruments with a maturity date of more than 12 months. The term **commercial paper** (see Chapter 3, Section 2.1.2) is used for instruments with a shorter maturity. Only companies with high credit ratings can issue bonds with a maturity greater than ten years at an acceptable cost.

Most corporate bonds are listed on stock exchanges, but the majority of trading in most developed markets takes place in the OTC market – that is directly between market counterparties.

4.1 Features of Corporate Bonds

There is a wide variety of corporate bonds and they can often be differentiated by looking at some of their key features, such as:

- security; and
- redemption provisions.

4.1.1 Bond Security

When a company is seeking to raise new funds by way of a bond issue, it will often have to offer **security** to provide the investor with some guarantee for the repayment of the bond. In this context, security usually means some form of charge over the issuer's assets (eg, its property or trade assets) so that, if the issuer defaults, the bondholders have a claim on those assets before other creditors (and so can regard their borrowings as safer than if there were no security). In some cases, the security takes the form of a third-party guarantee – for example, a guarantee by a bank that, if the issuer defaults, the bank will repay the bondholders.

The greater the security offered, the lower the cost of borrowing should be.

The security offered may be fixed or floating. Fixed security implies that specific assets (eg, a building) of the company are charged as security for the loan. A floating charge means that the general assets of the company are offered as security for the loan; this might include cash at the bank, trade debtors or stock.

4.1.2 Redemption Provisions

In some cases, a corporate bond will have a **call provision**, which gives the issuer the option to buy back all or part of the issue before maturity.

This is attractive to the issuer as it gives it the option to refinance the bond (ie, replace it with one at a lower rate of interest) when interest rates are lower than the coupon currently being paid. This is a disadvantage, however, to the investor, who will probably demand a higher yield as compensation.

Call provisions can take various forms. There may be a requirement for the issuer to redeem a specified amount at regular intervals. This is known as a **sinking fund** requirement.

Some bonds are issued with **put provisions**; these give the bondholder the right to require the issuer to redeem early, on a set date or between specific dates. This makes the bond attractive to investors and may increase the chances of selling a bond issue in the first instance. It does, however, increase the issuer's risk that it will have to refinance the bond at an inconvenient time.

4.2 Types of Corporate Debt

There is a large variety of corporate debt being issued and traded. Some of the main types are described below.

4.2.1 Medium-Term Notes (MTNs)

MTNs are standard corporate bonds with maturities ranging usually from nine months to five years, though the term is also applied to instruments with maturities as long as 30 years. How MTNs differ from other debt instruments is that they are offered to investors continually over a period of time by an agent of the issuer, instead of in a single tranche of one sizeable underwritten issue.

The market originated in the US to close the funding gap between commercial paper and long-term bonds.

4.2.2 Fixed Rate Bonds

The key features of fixed rate bonds have already been described above. Essentially, they have fixed coupons which are paid either half-yearly or annually, and predetermined redemption dates.

4.2.3 Floating Rate Notes (FRNs)

FRNs are bonds that have variable rates of interest.

The rate of interest will be linked to a benchmark rate such as the London interbank offered rate (LIBOR). This is the rate of interest at which banks will lend to one another in London, and is often used as a basis for financial instrument cash flows.

An FRN will usually pay interest at LIBOR (or another benchmark rate) plus a quoted margin or spread.

4.2.4 Convertible Bonds

Convertible bonds are issued by companies. They give the investor holding the bond two possible choices:

- to simply collect the interest payments and then the repayment of the bond on maturity; or

- to convert the bond into a predefined number of ordinary shares in the issuing company, on a set date or dates, or between a range of set dates, prior to the bond's maturity.

The attractions to the investor are:

- If the company prospers, its share price will rise and, if it does so sufficiently, conversion may lead to capital gains.
- If the company hits problems, the investor will retain the bond – interest will be earned and, as bondholder, the investor would rank ahead of existing shareholders if the company goes out of business. (Of course, if the company is seriously insolvent and the bond Is unsecured, the bondholder might still not be repaid, but this is a more remote possibility than that of a full loss as a shareholder.)

For the company, relatively cheap finance is acquired. Investors will pay a higher price for a bond that is convertible because of the possibility of a capital gain. However, the prospect of dilution of current shareholder interests, as convertible bondholders exercise their options, has to be borne in mind.

4.2.5 Zero Coupon Bonds (ZCBs)

ZCBs pay no interest. As seen, 'coupon' is an alternative term for the interest payment on a bond. The example below illustrates why a ZCB may be attractive.

Example

Imagine that the issuer of a bond (Example plc) offered you the opportunity to purchase a bond with the following features:

- €100 nominal value.
- Issued today.
- Redeems at its par value (that is €100 nominal value) in five years.
- Pays no interest.

Would you be interested in purchasing the bond?

It is tempting to say no – who would want to buy a bond that pays no interest?

However, there is no requirement to pay the par value – a logical investor would presumably happily pay something less than the par value, for example €60. The difference between the price paid of €60 and the par value of €100 recouped after five years would provide the investor with their return of €40 over five years.

As the example illustrates, these ZCBs are issued at a **discount to their par value** and they repay, or redeem, at par value. All of the return is provided in the form of capital growth rather than income and, as a result, it may be treated differently for tax purposes.

5. Asset-Backed Securities (ABSs)

Learning Objective

5.2.1 Know the definitions and features of the following types of bond: asset-backed securities

There is a large group of bonds that trade under the overall heading of 'asset-backed securities'.

These are bundled securities, so called because they are marketable securities that result from the bundling or packaging together of a set of non-marketable assets.

The assets in this pool, or bundle, range from mortgages and credit card debt to accounts receivable. The largest market is for mortgage-backed securities, which became known worldwide as a result of the sub-prime collapse in the US.

Mortgage-backed bonds are created by bundling together a set of mortgages and then issuing bonds that are backed by these assets. These bonds are sold on to investors, who receive interest payments until they are redeemed.

Creating a bond in this way is known as **securitisation**, and it began in the US in 1970 when the government first issued **mortgage certificates**, a security representing ownership of a pool of mortgages. As they were issued by government agencies, they carried guarantees and little risk and so were attractive to investors. This process spread, with banks using them to finance their mortgage-lending, generally issuing bonds representing ownership of a pool of mortgages with sound credit quality. Eventually the appetite for bonds with lower credit quality and the potential for greater returns grew, and banks started to issue mortgage bonds backed by sub-prime loans.

The way in which securitisation operates can be seen by looking at mortgage-backed bonds as an example in the following simplified diagram:

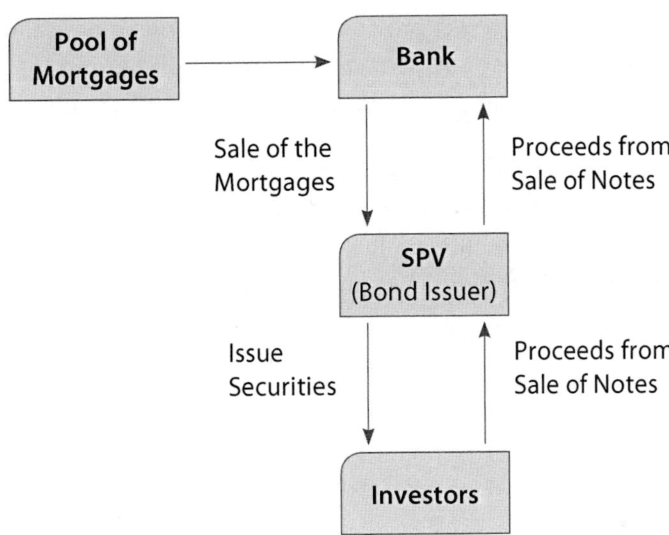

A set of mortgages packaged together by a bank is sold to a new company specifically set up for that purpose: a **special purpose vehicle** (**SPV**). The SPV will then issue bonds which will have the security of the original mortgages, along with different forms of credit enhancement, such as guarantees from the bank, insurance and over-collateralisation.

The SPV then issues to investors a range of bonds with different levels of security, each of which will have a rating from a credit rating agency. The bank receives the proceeds of the sale, which it can then use to finance other lending. The investor receives a bond that has the security of asset backing and credit enhancements and on which they will receive periodic interest payments until its eventual repayment.

As we can see from this process, the advantages to the bank are:

- Total funding available to the bank is increased by accessing capital markets rather than being dependent solely on its traditional deposit base.
- The mortgages are removed from its balance sheet and its risk exposure is diversified to another lender.
- Its liquidity position is helped, as the term to maturity of a mortgage may be 25 years and the securitisation issue replaces the financing that may have come from deposits that can be withdrawn at short notice.

From the investor's point of view, mortgage-backed bonds offer the following benefits:

- It is a marketable asset-backed instrument to invest in.
- Original mortgages will provide good security if well diversified and equivalent in terms of quality, terms and conditions.
- Credit enhancements make the securitised bonds a better credit risk.

A significant advantage of asset-backed securities is that they bring together a pool of financial assets that otherwise could not easily be traded in their existing form. The pooling together of a large portfolio of these illiquid assets converts them into instruments that may be offered and sold freely in the capital markets.

Their drawback was brought vividly to light in the sub-prime crisis. In normal circumstances, a pool of mortgages with high credit quality will provide a diversified spread of risk for bond investors. What happened in the sub-prime crisis is that poor quality (or sub-prime) mortgages were added to the mortgage pool, which left them vulnerable to the downturn in the US property market.

The result saw bond prices collapse and banks take huge losses as the downturn in the property market hit their own mortgage book and because of the guarantees provided to the SPVs. The bonds had been sold to investors worldwide, who saw sharp falls in the value of their holdings, including many that were judged as safe by the ratings agencies.

6. International Bonds

Learning Objective

5.2.1 Know the definitions and features of the following types of bond: domestic; foreign; eurobond

In this section we will consider the main types of international bonds that are issued.

6.1 Domestic and Foreign Bonds

Bonds can be categorised geographically. A **domestic bond** is issued by a domestic issuer into the domestic market, for example, a UK company issuing bonds, denominated in sterling, to UK investors.

In contrast, a **foreign bond** is issued by an overseas entity into a domestic market and is denominated in the domestic currency. Examples of a foreign bond are a German company issuing a sterling bond to UK investors or a US dollar bond issued in the US by a non-US company.

6.2 Eurobonds

Eurobonds are large international bond issues often made by governments and multinational companies.

The eurobond market developed in the early 1970s to accommodate the recycling of substantial Organisation of Petroleum Exporting Countries (OPEC) US dollar revenues from Middle East oil sales at a time when US financial institutions were subject to a ceiling on the rate of interest that could be paid on dollar deposits. Since then it has grown exponentially into the world's largest market for longer-term capital, as a result of the corresponding growth in world trade and even more significant growth in international capital flows. Most of the activity is concentrated in London.

Often issued in a number of financial centres simultaneously, the one defining characteristic of eurobonds is that they are **denominated in a currency different from that of the financial centre or centres from which they are issued**. An example might be a German company issuing either a euro, a dollar or a sterling bond to Japanese investors.

In this respect, the term eurobond is a bit of a misnomer as eurobond issues and the currencies in which they are denominated are not restricted to those of European financial centres or countries.

The 'euro' prefix simply originates from the depositing of US dollars in the European eurodollar market and has been applied to the eurobond market since then. So, a euro sterling bond issue is one denominated in sterling and issued outside the UK, though not necessarily in a European financial centre. Eurobonds issued by companies often do not provide any underlying collateral, or security, to the bondholders but are almost always rated by a credit rating agency.

To prevent the interests of these bondholders being subordinated, or made inferior, to those of any subsequent bond issues, the company makes a 'negative pledge' clause. This prevents the company making any secured bond issues, or issues which confer greater seniority (ie, priority) or entitlement to the company's assets in the event of its liquidation, unless an equivalent level of security is provided to existing bondholders.

The eurobond market offers a number of advantages over a domestic bond market that make it an attractive way for companies to raise capital, including:

- a choice of innovative products to more precisely meet issuers' needs;
- the ability to tap potential lenders internationally, rather than just domestically;
- anonymity to investors as issues are made in bearer form;
- gross interest payments to investors;
- lower funding costs due to the competitive nature and greater liquidity of the market;
- the ability to make bond issues at short notice; and
- less regulation and disclosure.

Most eurobonds are issued as conventional bonds (or 'straights'), with a fixed nominal value, fixed coupon and known redemption date. Other common types include FRNs, ZCBs, convertible bonds and dual-currency bonds – but they can also assume a wide range of other innovative features.

7. Yields

Learning Objective

5.2.2 Be able to calculate the flat yield of a bond

Yields are a measure of the returns to be earned on bonds.

The coupon reflects the interest rate payable on the nominal or principal amount. However, an investor may have paid a different amount to purchase the bond, so a method of calculating the true return is needed. The return, as a percentage of the cost price, which a bond offers is often referred to as the bond's **yield**.

The interest paid on a bond as a percentage of its market price is referred to as the **flat**, or **running**, yield.

The flat yield is calculated by taking the annual coupon and dividing by the bond's price, and then multiplying by 100 to obtain a percentage.

The bond's price is typically stated as the price payable to purchase US$100 nominal value or whichever currency the bond is dealt in.

Example

Staying with our example from Section 2.1 of a US Treasury bond with a 7.5% coupon that is due to be redeemed at par in 2024 and is currently priced at US$146.80, this would have a flat yield of:

$$(7.5 \div 146.80) \times 100 = 5.11\%$$

The interest earned on a bond is only one part of its total return, however, as the investor may also either make a capital gain or a loss on the bond if they hold it until redemption.

Staying with the example of the US Treasury stock used above, it was purchased for US$146.80 but will only repay US$100 when it is repaid in 2024. So if an investor holds the bond until repayment, they will receive an attractive return each year but will make a capital loss, and so a measure is needed to take this into account.

5

The **redemption yield** is a measure that incorporates both the income and capital return – assuming the investor holds the bond until its maturity – into one figure.

7.1 Yield Curve

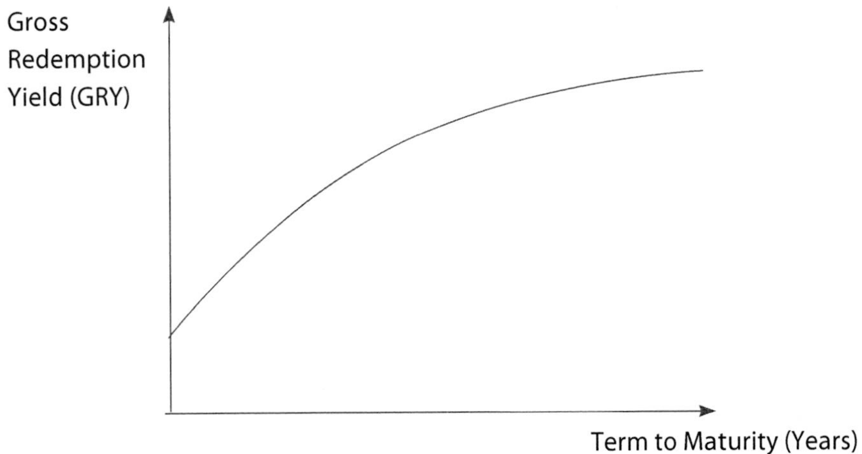

The **yield curve**, as shown in the diagram above, is a way of illustrating the different rates of interest that can be obtained in the market for similar debt instruments with different maturity dates. Although yield curves can assume a range of different shapes, in normal market circumstances the yield curve is described as being 'positive', ie, it slopes upward, as in the diagram.

The rationale for this is that the longer an investor is going to tie up capital, the higher the rate of interest they will demand to compensate themselves for the greater risk, and opportunity cost, on the capital they have invested.

End of Chapter Questions

Think of an answer for each question and refer to the appropriate section for confirmation.

1. What will be the impact of a fall in interest rates on bond prices?
Answer Reference: Section 2.2

2. What is the function of a call provision when attached to a bond?
Answer Reference: Section 4.1.2

3. What options do a convertible bond give to an investor?
Answer Reference: Section 4.2.4

4. What type of bond does not pay interest?
Answer Reference: Section 4.2.5

5. You have a holding of £1,000 Treasury 5% stock 2028 which is priced at £104. What is its flat yield?
Answer Reference: Section 7

Chapter Six

Derivatives

6

This syllabus area will provide approximately 6 of the 50 examination questions

1. Overview of Derivatives

Derivatives are not a new concept – they have been around for hundreds of years. Their origins can be traced back to agricultural markets, where farmers needed a mechanism to guard against price fluctuations caused by gluts of produce, and merchants wanted to guard against shortages that might arise from periods of drought.

So, in order to fix the price of agricultural produce in advance of harvest time, farmers and merchants would enter into **forward contracts**. These set the price at which a stated amount of a commodity would be delivered between a farmer and a merchant (termed the 'counterparties' to the trade) at a pre-specified future date.

These early derivative contracts introduced an element of certainty into commerce and gained immense popularity. They led to the opening of the world's first derivatives exchange in 1848, the Chicago Board of Trade (CBOT).

Modern **commodity markets** have their roots in this trading of agricultural products. Commodity markets are where raw or primary products are exchanged or traded on regulated exchanges. They are bought and sold in **standardised contracts** – a standardised contract is one when not only the amount and timing of the contract conforms to the exchange's norm, but also the quality and form of the underlying asset – for example, the dryness of wheat or the purity of metals.

Commodities are sold by producers (eg, farmers, mining companies and oil companies) and purchased by consumers (eg, food manufacturers and industrial goods manufacturers). Much of the buying and selling is undertaken via commodity derivatives, which also offer the ability for producers and consumers to hedge their exposure to price movements. However, there is also substantial trading in commodities (and their derivatives) undertaken by financial firms and speculators seeking to make profits by correctly predicting market movements.

Today, derivatives trading also takes place in financial instruments, indices, metals, energy and a wide range of other assets.

1.1 Uses of Derivatives

Learning Objective

6.1.1 Know the uses and application of derivatives

6.4.1 Understand the following terms: OTC; exchange-traded

A derivative is a financial instrument whose price is based on the price of another asset, known as the 'underlying'. The underlying could be a financial asset, a commodity, a currency or an index. Examples of financial assets include bonds and shares, and commodities include oil, gold, silver, corn and wheat.

As we will see later in this chapter, the trading of derivatives can take place either directly between counterparties or on an organised exchange. When trading takes place directly between counterparties it is referred to as **over-the-counter (OTC)** trading, and when it takes place on an exchange, such as the Chicago Mercantile Exchange (CME), the derivatives are referred to as being **exchange-traded**.

Derivatives play a major role in the investment management of many large portfolios and funds, and are used for hedging, anticipating future cash flows, asset allocation change and arbitrage. Each of these uses is expanded on briefly below:

- **Hedging.** This is a technique employed by portfolio managers to reduce portfolio risk, such as the impact of adverse price movements on a portfolio's value. This could be achieved by buying or selling futures contracts, buying put options or selling call options.
- **Anticipating future cash flows.** Closely linked to the idea of hedging, if a portfolio manager expects to receive a large inflow of cash to be invested in a particular asset, then futures can be used to fix the price at which it will be bought and offset the risk that prices will have risen by the time the cash flow is received.
- **Asset allocation changes.** Changes to the asset allocation of a fund, whether to take advantage of anticipated short-term directional market movements or to implement a change in strategy, can be made more swiftly and less expensively using derivatives such as futures than by actually buying and selling securities within the underlying portfolio.
- **Arbitrage.** The process of deriving a risk-free profit from simultaneously buying and selling the same asset in two different markets, when a price difference between the two exists. If the price of a derivative and its underlying asset are mismatched, then the portfolio manager may be able to profit from this pricing anomaly.
- **Speculation.** Involves assuming additional risk (betting) in an effort to make, or increase, profits in the portfolio.

The vast majority of derivatives take one of four forms: forwards, futures, options and swaps.

2. Futures

Learning Objective

6.2.1 Know the definition and function of a future

6.4.1 Understand the following terms: long; short; open; close

2.1 Development of Futures

As mentioned above, the **CBOT opened the world's first derivatives exchange in 1848**. The exchange soon developed a **futures contract** that enabled standardised qualities and quantities of grain to be traded for a fixed future price on a stated delivery date. Unlike the **forward contracts** that preceded it, the futures contract could itself be traded. These futures contracts have subsequently been extended to a wide variety of commodities and are offered by an ever-increasing number of derivatives exchanges.

It was not until 1975 that CBOT introduced the world's first **financial futures contract**. This set the scene for the exponential growth in product innovation and the volume of futures trading that followed.

2.2 Definition of a Future

Derivatives provide a mechanism by which the price of assets or commodities can be traded in the future at a price agreed today, without the full value of this transaction being exchanged or settled at the outset.

A future is a legally binding agreement between a buyer and a seller. The buyer agrees to pay a pre-specified amount for the delivery of a particular pre-specified quantity of an asset at a pre-specified future date. The seller agrees to deliver the asset at the future date, in exchange for the pre-specified amount of money.

Example

A buyer might agree with a seller to pay US$55 per barrel for 1,000 barrels of crude oil in three months' time. The buyer might be an electricity-generating company wanting to fix the price it will have to pay for the oil to use in its oil-fired power stations, and the seller might be an oil company wanting to fix the sales price of some of its future oil production.

A futures contract has two distinct features:

- It is **exchange-traded** – for example, on the derivatives exchanges like LIFFE (London International Financial Futures and Options Exchange) or the IntercontinentalExchange (ICE).
- It is dealt on **standardised terms** – the exchange specifies the quality of the underlying asset, the quantity underlying each contract, the future date and the delivery location. Only the price is open to negotiation. In the above example, the oil quality will be based on the oil field from which it originates (eg, Brent crude – from the Brent oil field in the North Sea), the quantity is 1,000 barrels, the date is three months ahead and the location might be the port of Rotterdam in the Netherlands.

2.3 Futures Terminology

Derivatives markets have specialised terminology that is important to understand.

Staying with the example above, the electricity company is the buyer of the contract, agreeing to purchase 1,000 barrels of crude oil at US$55 per barrel for delivery in three months. The buyer is said to go **long** of the contract, while the seller (the oil company in the above example) is described as going **short**. Entering into the transaction is known as **opening the trade** and the eventual delivery of the crude oil will **close-out** the trade.

The definitions of these key terms that the futures market uses are as follows:

- **Long** – the term used for the position taken by the buyer of the future. The person who is 'long' in the contract is committed to buying the underlying asset at the pre-agreed price on the specified future date.
- **Short** – the position taken by the seller of the future. The seller is committed to delivering the underlying asset in exchange for the pre-agreed price on the specified future date.
- **Open** – the initial trade. A market participant opens a trade when it first enters into a future. It could be buying a future (opening a long position) or selling a future (opening a short position).

- **Close** – the physical assets underlying most futures that are opened do not end up being delivered: they are closed-out instead. For example, an opening buyer will almost invariably avoid delivery by making a closing sale before the delivery date. If the buyer does not close-out, he will pay the agreed sum and receive the underlying asset. This might be something the buyer is keen to avoid, for example because the buyer is actually a financial institution simply speculating on the price of the underlying asset using futures.

3. Options

Learning Objective

6.3.1 Know the definition and function of an option

6.3.2 Understand the following terms: calls; puts

6.4.1 Understand the following terms: holder; writing; premium; covered; naked

3.1 Development of Options

Options did not really start to flourish until two US academics produced an option pricing model in 1973 that allowed them to be readily priced. This paved the way for the creation of standardised options contracts and the opening of the **Chicago Board Options Exchange (CBOE)** in the same year. This in turn led to an explosion in product innovation and the creation of other options exchanges, such as LIFFE.

Options can also be traded off-exchange, or OTC, where the contract specification determined by the parties is bespoke.

3.2 Definition of an Option

An option gives a buyer the right, but not the obligation, to buy or sell a specified quantity of an underlying asset at a pre-agreed exercise price, on or before a pre-specified future date or between two specified dates. The seller, in exchange for the payment of a premium, grants the option to the buyer.

3.3 Options Terminology

There are two classes of options:

- A **call option** is when the buyer has the right to buy the asset at the exercise price, if they choose to. The seller is obliged to deliver if the buyer exercises the option.
- A **put option** is when the buyer has the right to sell the underlying asset at the exercise price. The seller of the put option is obliged to take delivery and pay the exercise price, if the buyer exercises the option.

The buyers of options are the owners of those options. They are also referred to as **holders**.

The sellers of options are referred to as the **writers** of those options. Their sale is also referred to as **taking for the call** or **taking for the put**, depending on whether they receive a premium for selling a call option or a put option.

The **premium** is the money paid by the buyer to the writer at the beginning of the options contract; it is not refundable.

The following example of an options contract is intended to assist understanding of the way in which option contracts might be used.

Example

Suppose shares in Jersey plc are trading at US$3.24 and an investor buys a US$3.50 call for three months. The investor, Frank, has the right to buy Jersey shares from the writer of the option (another investor – Steve) at US$3.50 if he chooses, at any stage over the next three months.

If Jersey shares are below US$3.50 three months later (upon expiry), Frank will abandon the option and it will expire worthless, and Steve will keep the premium Frank paid him.

If they rise to, say, US$6.00 Frank will contact Steve and either:

- exercise the option (buy the shares at US$3.50 each and keep them, or sell them at US$6.00 per share); or
- persuade Steve to give him US$6.00 – US$3.50 = US$2.50 per share to settle the transaction.

If Frank paid a premium of 42 cents to Steve, what is Frank's maximum loss and what level does Jersey plc have to reach for Frank to make a profit?

The most Frank can lose is 42 cents, the premium he has paid. If the Jersey plc shares rise above US$3.50 + 42 cents, or US$3.92, then Frank makes a profit. If the shares rise to US$3.51 then Frank will exercise his right to buy – better to make a cent and cut his losses to 41 cents than lose the whole 42 cents.

The most Steve can gain is the premium, ie, 42 cents. Steve's potential loss, however, is theoretically unlimited, unless he actually holds the underlying shares.

Staying with that example, we can look at the terms 'covered' and 'naked'. The writer of the option is hoping that the investor will not exercise his right to buy the underlying shares and then he can simply pocket the premium. This obviously presents a risk because if the price does rise then the writer will need to find the shares to meet his obligation. He may not have the shares to deliver and may have to buy these in the market, in which case his position is referred to as being **naked** (ie, he does not have the underlying asset – the shares). Alternatively, he may hold the shares, and his position would be referred to as **covered**.

4. Swaps

Learning Objective

6.6.1 Know the definition and function of an interest rate swap

6.6.2 Know the definition and function of a credit default swap

4.1 Description of Swaps

A swap is an agreement to exchange one set of cash flows for another. Swaps are a form of OTC derivative and are negotiated between the parties to meet their different needs, so each tends to be unique.

4.2 Interest-Rate Swaps

Interest rate swaps are the most common form of swaps. They involve an exchange of interest payments and are usually constructed whereby one leg of the swap is a payment of a fixed rate of interest and the other leg is a payment of a floating rate of interest.

They are usually used to hedge exposure to interest rate changes and can be easily appreciated by looking at an example.

Example

Company A is embarking on a three-year project to build and equip a new manufacturing plant, and borrows funds to finance the cost. Because of its size and credit status, it has no choice but to borrow at variable rates. It can reasonably estimate what additional returns its new plant will generate but, because the interest it is paying will be variable, it is exposed to the risk that the project may turn out to be uneconomic if interest rates rise unexpectedly.

If the company could secure fixed-rate finance, it could remove the risk of interest rate variations and more accurately predict the returns it can make from its investment.

To do this, Company A could enter into an interest rate swap with an investment bank. Under the terms of the swap, Company A pays a fixed rate to the investment bank and in exchange receives an amount of interest calculated on a variable rate. With the amount it receives from the investment bank, it then has the funds to settle its variable rate lending, even if rates increase. In this way, it has hedged its concerns about interest rates rising.

The two exchanges of cash flow are known as the **legs** of the swap and the amounts to be exchanged are calculated by reference to a **notional amount**. The notional amount in the above example would be the amount that Company A has borrowed to fund its project.

Typically, one party will pay an amount based on a fixed rate to the other party, who will pay back an amount of interest that is variable and usually based on a benchmark rate such as LIBOR (the London Interbank Offered Rate – a rate that is established and published daily). The variable rate will usually be set as LIBOR plus, say, 0.5% and will be reset quarterly. The variable rate is often described as the 'floating' rate.

4.3 Credit Default Swaps (CDSs)

In recent years there has been significant growth in the use of credit derivatives, of which a credit default swap (CDS) is just one example.

Credit derivatives are instruments whose value depends on agreed credit events relating to a third-party company, for example, changes to the credit rating of that company, or an increase in that company's cost of funds in the market, or credit events relating to it. Credit events are typically defined as including a material default, bankruptcy, a significant fall in an asset's value, or debt restructuring for a specified reference asset.

The purpose of credit derivatives is to enable an organisation to protect itself against unwanted credit exposure by passing that exposure on to someone else. Credit derivatives can also be used to increase credit exposure in return for income.

Although a CDS has the word 'swap' in its name, it is not like other types of swaps, which are based on the exchange of cash flows. A CDS is actually more like an option. In a credit default swap, the party buying credit protection makes a periodic payment (or pays an up-front fee) to a second party, the seller. In return, the buyer receives an agreed compensation if there is a credit event relating to some third party or parties. If such a credit event occurs, the seller makes a predetermined payment to the buyer, and the CDS then terminates.

5. Derivatives Markets

Learning Objective

6.5.1 Know the function of a derivatives exchange and the products traded

As we saw earlier, there are two distinct groups of derivatives, differentiated by how they are traded. These are OTC derivatives and exchange-traded derivatives.

OTC derivatives are ones that are negotiated and traded privately between parties without the use of an exchange. Interest rate swaps are just one of a number of products that are traded in this way.

The OTC market is the larger of the two in terms of value of contracts traded daily. Trading takes place predominantly in Europe and, particularly, in the UK. (Note: there is considerable activity taking place at the moment to move OTC trading on exchange in response to regulatory concerns about the risks posed by OTC derivative trading.)

Exchange-traded derivatives are ones that have standardised features and can therefore be traded on an organised exchange, such as single stock or index derivatives. The role of the exchange is to provide a marketplace for trading to take place but also to provide some sort of guarantee that the trade will eventually be settled. It does this by placing an intermediary (the **central counterparty** or CCP) between the parties to each trade and by requiring participants to post a **margin**, which is a proportion of the value of the trade, for all transactions that are entered into.

Examples of some leading derivatives exchanges are shown below.

CME	• The main derivatives exchange in the US is the CME Group, which was formed out of the merger in 2006 of the CBOT and the CME. It is the world's largest and most diverse derivatives exchange. • It operates the CME, the CBOT, NYMEX (New York Mercantile Exchange) and COMEX derivatives exchanges.
ICE	• ICE operates a number of exchanges and trading platforms, including futures exchanges in the US, Canada, Europe and Singapore as well as equity options exchanges.
LME	• The London Metal Exchange (LME) has been operating for over 130 years. Although it is based in London, it is a global market with an international membership and with more than 95% of its business coming from overseas. • The LME trades derivatives on non-precious, non-ferrous metals, such as copper, aluminium and zinc. Trading is predominantly by open outcry on the floor of the exchange.
Eurex	• Eurex is based in Frankfurt, Germany. Its principal products are German bond futures and options, the most well-known of which are contracts on the Bund (the German government bond). It also trades index products for a range of European markets.

5.1 Investing in Derivatives Markets

Learning Objective

6.5.2 Know the advantages and disadvantages of investing in the derivatives and commodity markets

Having looked at various types of derivatives and their main uses, we can summarise some of the main advantages and disadvantages of investing in derivatives.

Advantages

- Enables producers and consumers of goods to agree the price of a commodity today for future delivery, which can remove the uncertainty of what price will be achieved for the producer and the risk of lack of supply for the consumer.
- Enables investors and portfolio managers to hedge (reduce) the risk associated with a portfolio of investments.
- Enables investment firms to hedge the risk associated with a portfolio or an individual stock.
- Offers the ability to speculate on a wide range of assets and markets to make large bets on price movements using the geared nature of derivatives.

Drawbacks and Risks

- Some types of derivatives investing can involve the investor losing more than their initial outlay and, in some cases, facing potentially unlimited losses.
- Derivatives markets thrive on price volatility, meaning that professional investment skills and experience are required.
- In the OTC markets, there is a risk that a counterparty may default on their obligations, and so it requires great attention to detail in terms of counterparty risk assessment, documentation and the taking of collateral.

End of Chapter Questions

Think of an answer for each question and refer to the appropriate section for confirmation.

1. What are the main investment uses of derivatives?
Answer Reference: Section 1

2. What are the two key differences between a future and an option?
Answer Reference: Sections 2.2 and 3.2

3. What is the seller of a future known as?
Answer Reference: Section 2.3

4. What is an investor who enters into a contract for the delivery of an asset in three months' time known as?
Answer Reference: Section 2.3

5. What name is given to the seller of an option?
Answer Reference: Section 3.3

6. What type of option gives the holder the right to sell an asset?
Answer Reference: Section 3.3

7. What is the price paid for an option known as and who is it paid to?
Answer Reference: Section 3.3

8. What is an interest-rate swap?
Answer Reference: Section 4.2

9. Which type of derivative is not exchange-traded?
Answer Reference: Section 5

Chapter Seven

Investment Funds

This syllabus area will provide approximately 7 of the 50 examination questions

1. Overview of Investment Funds

When investors decide to invest in a particular asset class, such as equities, there are two ways they can do it: direct investment or indirect investment.

Direct investment is when an individual personally buys shares in a company, such as buying shares in Apple, the technology giant.

Indirect investment is when an individual buys a stake in an investment fund, such as a mutual fund that invests in the shares of a range of different types of companies, perhaps including Apple.

Achieving an adequate spread of investments through holding direct investments can require a significant amount of money and, as a result, many investors find indirect investment very attractive.

There is a range of funds available that pool the resources of a large number of investors to provide access to a range of investments. These pooled funds are known as **collective investment schemes (CISs)**, funds, or collective investment vehicles. (The term 'collective investment scheme' is an internationally recognised one, but investment funds are also very well-known by other names, such as mutual funds, unit trusts or open-ended investment companies [OEIC]).

An investor is likely to come across a range of different types of investment funds, as many are now established in one country and then marketed internationally. Funds that are established in Europe and marketed internationally are often labelled as **'undertakings for collective investment in transferable securities' (UCITS)** funds, meaning that they comply with the rules of the EU UCITS directive. The UCITS branding is seen as a measure of quality that makes them acceptable for sale in many countries in the Middle East and Asia.

The main European centre for establishing funds that are to be marketed internationally is Luxembourg, where investment funds are often structured as an OEIC known as a Société d'Investissement à Capital Variable (SICAV).

Other popular centres for the establishment of investment funds that are marketed globally include the UK, Ireland and Jersey, where the legal structure is likely to be either an OEIC or a unit trust.

The international nature of the investment funds business can be seen by looking at the funds authorised for sale in Bahrain, which probably has the widest range of funds available in the Gulf region with over 2,700 funds registered for sale. Some of these are domiciled in Bahrain, but many are funds from international fund management houses such as BlackRock, Fidelity and J.P. Morgan. They include SICAVs (see Section 2.2.1), ICVCs (investment companies with variable capital – see Section 2.2.3) and unit trusts from a range of internationally recognised firms.

1.1 The Benefits of Collective Investment

Learning Objective

7.1.1 Understand the benefits of collective investment

CISs pool the resources of a large number of investors, with the aim of pursuing a common investment objective.

This pooling of funds brings a number of benefits, including:

- economies of scale;
- diversification;
- access to professional investment management;
- access to geographical markets, asset classes or investment strategies which might otherwise be inaccessible to the individual investor;
- in some cases, the benefit of regulatory oversight; and
- in some cases, tax deferral.

The value of shares and most other investments can fall as well as rise. Some might fall spectacularly, such as when Enron collapsed or when banks had to be bailed out during the recent credit crisis. However, when an investor holds a diversified pool of investments in a portfolio, the risk of single constituent investments falling spectacularly could be offset by outperformance on the part of other investments. In other words, risk is lessened when the investor holds a diversified portfolio of investments (of course, the opportunity of a startling outperformance is also diversified away – but many investors are happy with this if it reduces their risk of total or significant loss).

An investor needs a substantial amount of money before he or she can create a diversified portfolio of investments directly. If an investor has only US$3,000 to invest, and wants to buy the shares of 30 different companies, each investment would be US$100. This would result in a large amount of the US$3,000 being spent on commission, since there will be minimum commission rates of, say, US$10 on each purchase.

Alternatively, an investment of US$3,000 might go into an investment fund with, say, 80 different investments, but, because the investment is being pooled with that of lots of other investors, the commission as a proportion of the fund is very small.

An investment fund might also be invested in shares from many different sectors; this achieves diversification from an industry perspective (thereby reducing the risk of investing in a number of shares whose performance is closely correlated). Alternatively, it may invest in a variety of bonds. Some investment funds put limited amounts of investment into bank deposits and even into other investment funds.

The other main rationale for investing collectively is to access the investing skills of the fund manager. Fund managers follow their chosen markets closely and will carefully consider what to buy and whether to keep or sell their chosen investments. Few investors have the skill, time or inclination to do this as effectively themselves.

However, fund managers do not manage portfolios for nothing. They might charge investors' fees to become involved in their CIS (entry fees or initial charges) or to leave (exit charges), plus annual management fees. These fees are needed to cover the fund managers' salaries, technology, research, their dealing, settlement and risk management systems, and to provide a profit.

1.2 Investment Strategies

Learning Objective

7.1.2 Know the difference between active and passive management

There is a wide range of funds with many different investment objectives and investment styles. Each of these funds has an investment portfolio managed by a fund manager according to a clearly stated set of objectives.

An example of an objective might be to invest in the shares of UK companies with above-average potential for capital growth and to outperform the FTSE (Financial Times Stock Exchange) All-Share index. Other funds' objectives could be to maximise income or to achieve steady growth in capital and income.

In each case, it will also be clear what the fund manager will invest in; for example, shares and/or bonds and/or property and/or cash or money instruments; and whether derivatives will be used to hedge currency or other market risks.

It is also important to understand the investment style the fund manager adopts. Investment styles refer to the fund manager's approach to choosing investments and meeting the fund's objectives. In this section we will look at the difference between active and passive management.

1.2.1 Passive Management

Passive management is seen in those types of investment funds that are often described as index-tracker funds. **Index-tracking**, or **indexation**, involves constructing a portfolio in such a way that it will track, or mimic, the performance of a recognised index.

Indexation is undertaken on the assumption that securities markets are efficiently priced and cannot therefore be consistently outperformed. Consequently, no attempt is made to forecast future events or outperform the broader market.

The advantages of employing indexation are that:

- Relatively few active portfolio managers consistently outperform benchmark indices.
- Once set up, passive portfolios are generally less expensive to run than active portfolios, given a lower ratio of staff to funds managed and lower portfolio turnover.

The disadvantages of adopting indexation, however, include the following:

- Performance is affected by the need to manage cash flows, rebalance the portfolio to replicate changes in index constituent weightings and adjust the portfolio for stocks coming into, and falling out of, the index. This can lead to tracking error if the performance does not match that of the underlying index.
- Also most indices assume that dividends from constituent equities are reinvested on the ex-dividend (xd) date, whereas a passive fund can only invest dividends when they are received, up to six weeks after the share has been declared ex-dividend.
- Indexed portfolios may not meet all of an investor's objectives.
- Indexed portfolios follow the index down in bear markets.

1.2.2 Active Management

In contrast to passive management, active management seeks to outperform a predetermined benchmark over a specified time period. It does so by employing fundamental and technical analysis to assist in the forecasting of future events, which may be economic or specific to a company, so as to determine the portfolio's holdings and the timing of purchases and sales of securities. Actively managed funds usually have higher charges than those that are passively managed.

Two commonly used terms in this context are 'top-down' and 'bottom-up'. **Top-down** means that the manager focuses on economic and industry trends rather than the prospects of particular companies. **Bottom-up** means that the analysis of a company's net assets, future profitability and cash flow and other company-specific indicators is a priority.

Included in the bottom-up approach is a range of investment styles, including:

- **growth investing** – which is picking the shares of companies with present opportunities to grow significantly in the long term;
- **value investing** – which is picking the shares of companies that are undervalued relative to their present and future profits or cash flows;
- **momentum investing** – which is picking the shares whose share price is rising on the basis that this rise will continue;
- **contrarian investing** – the flip side of momentum investing, which involves picking shares that are out of favour and may have hidden value.

There is also a significant range of styles used by managers of hedge funds. (Hedge funds are considered in Section 5.)

1.2.3 Combining Active and Passive Management

Having considered both active and passive management, it should be noted that active and passive investment are not mutually exclusive.

Index-trackers and actively managed funds can be combined in what is known as **core-satellite management**. This is achieved by indexing, say, 70% to 80% of the portfolio's value (the core), so as to minimise the risk of underperformance, and then fine-tuning this by investing the remainder in a number of specialist actively managed funds or individual securities. This is the satellite element of the fund.

1.3 Authorised versus Unauthorised Funds

In most markets, some CISs are authorised, while others may be unauthorised or unregulated funds.

The way this usually operates is that, in order to sell a fund to investors, the fund group has to seek authorisation from that country's regulator. The approach adopted by the regulator will then depend on whether the fund is to be distributed to retail investors or only to experienced investors.

If a fund is to be sold to retail investors, the regulator will authorise only those schemes that are sufficiently diversified and that invest in a range of permitted assets. CISs that have been authorised in this way can be freely marketed to retail investors.

CISs that have not been authorised by the regulator cannot be marketed to the general public. These unauthorised vehicles are perfectly legal, but their marketing must be carried out subject to certain rules and, in some cases, only to certain types of investors, such as institutional investors.

2. Open-Ended Funds

Learning Objective

7.2.1 Know the characteristics and different types of open-ended fund/mutual fund: US; Europe

An open-ended fund is an investment fund that can issue and redeem shares at any time. Each investor has a pro rata share of the underlying portfolio and so will share in any growth of the fund. The value of each share is in proportion to the total value of the underlying investment portfolio.

If investors wish to invest in an open-ended fund, they approach the fund directly and provide the money they wish to invest. The fund can create new shares in response to this demand, issuing new shares or units to the investor at a price based on the value of the underlying portfolio. If investors decide to sell, they again approach the fund, which will redeem the shares and pay the investor the value of their shares, again based on the value of the underlying portfolio.

An open-ended fund can therefore expand and contract in size based on investor demand, which is why it is referred to as open-ended.

2.1 US Open-Ended Funds

The most well-known type of US investment fund is a **mutual fund**. Legally it is known as an 'open-end company' under federal securities laws. A mutual fund is one of three main types of investment fund in the US; the others are considered later in this chapter in the section on closed-ended funds.

Most mutual funds fall into one of three main categories:

- Money market funds.
- Bond funds, which are also called fixed income funds.
- Stock funds, which are also called equity funds.

2.1.1 Main Characteristics

Some of their key distinguishing characteristics include:

- The mutual fund can create and sell new shares to accommodate new investors.
- Investors buy mutual fund shares directly from the fund itself, rather than from other investors on a secondary market such as the NYSE (New York Stock Exchange) or NASDAQ (National Association of Securities Dealers Automated Quotations).
- The price that investors pay for mutual fund shares is based on the fund's **net asset value** (the **NAV**, which is the value of the underlying investment portfolio) plus any charges made by the fund.
- The investment portfolios of mutual funds are typically managed by separate entities known as investment advisers, who are registered with the Securities Exchange Commission (SEC), the US regulator.

2.1.2 Buying and Selling Mutual Fund Shares

Investors can place instructions to buy or sell shares in mutual funds by contacting the fund directly. However, in practice, most mutual fund shares are sold mainly through brokers, banks, financial planners or insurance agents.

The price that an investor will pay to buy shares or receive when they are redeemed is based on the **NAV** of the underlying portfolio. A mutual fund will value its portfolio daily in order to determine the value of its investment portfolio, and from this calculate the price at which investors will deal. The NAV is available from the fund, on its website and in the financial pages of major newspapers.

When an investor buys shares, they pay the current NAV per share plus any fee the fund imposes. When an investor sells their shares, the fund will pay them the NAV minus any charges made for redemption of the shares. All mutual funds will redeem or buy back an investor's shares on any business day and must send payment within seven days.

2.1.3 Fees and Expenses

Operating a mutual fund involves costs such as shareholder transaction costs, investment advisory fees, and marketing and distribution expenses. Mutual funds pass along these costs to investors by imposing charges. SEC rules require mutual funds to disclose both shareholder fees and operating expenses in a fee table near the front of a fund's prospectus.

Operating expenses refers to the costs involved in running the fund and are typically paid out of fund assets. Included within these costs are:

- **Management fees** – the costs of the investment adviser who manages the portfolio.

- **Distribution and service fees** – these are fees paid to cover the costs of marketing and selling fund shares including fees to brokers and others and the costs involved in responding to investor enquiries and providing information to investors.
- **Other expenses** – under this heading are all other charges incurred by the fund such as custody charges, legal and accounting expenses and other administrative expenses.

As well as disclosing these costs, mutual funds are also required to state the total annual fund operating expenses as a percentage of the fund's average net assets. This is known as the **expense ratio**, and helps investors make comparisons between funds.

As well as the costs that are involved in running a mutual fund, a fund may also impose **charges** when an investor buys, sells or switches mutual fund shares. The types of charges that are levied include:

- **Sales charge on purchases** – this is the amount payable when shares are bought and is sometimes referred to as a 'front-end load'. It is paid to the broker that sells the fund's shares. It is deducted from the amount to be invested so, for example, if you invest US$1,000 and there is a 5% front-end load, then only US$950 will be actually invested in the fund. Regulations restrict the maximum front-end charge to 8.5%.
- **Purchase fee** – this is a fee that funds sometimes charge to defray the costs of the purchase, and is payable to the mutual fund and not the broker.
- **Deferred sales charge** – this is a fee that is paid when shares are sold and is known as a 'back-end load'. This typically goes to the broker that sold the shares, and the amount payable decreases the longer the investor holds the shares, until a point is reached when the investor has held the shares for long enough that nothing is payable.
- **Redemption fee** – another type of fee that is paid when an investor sells their shares, but which is payable to the fund and not the broker.
- **Exchange fee** – this is a fee that some funds impose when an investor wants to switch to another fund within the same group or family of funds.

When a fund charges a front-end sales load, the amount payable will be lower for larger investments. The amount that needs to be invested needs to exceed what are commonly referred to as **breakpoints**. It is up to each fund to determine how they will calculate whether an investor is entitled to receive a breakpoint, and regulatory requirements forbid advisers selling shares of an amount that is just below the fund's sales load breakpoint simply to earn a higher commission.

Some funds are described as 'no-load', which means that the fund does not charge any type of sales load. They may, however, charge fees that are not sales loads, such as purchase fees, redemption fees, exchange fees and account fees. No-load funds will also have operating expenses.

2.1.4 Classes of Shares

Many mutual funds have more than one class of shares. While the underlying investment portfolio remains the same for all of the different classes, each will have different distribution arrangements and fees.

Some of the most common mutual fund share classes offered to individual investors are:

- **Class A shares** – these typically impose a front-end load but have lower annual expenses.

- **Class B shares** – these do not impose a front-end load and instead may impose a deferred sales load along with operating expenses.
- **Class C shares** – these have operating expenses and a front-end load or back-end load but this will be lower than for the other classes. They will typically have higher annual operating expenses than the other share classes.

2.1.5 Other Characteristics

The tax treatment of a US fund varies depending upon its type.

For example, some funds are classed as tax-exempt funds, such as a municipal bond fund where all of the dividends are exempt from federal and sometimes state income tax, although tax is due on any capital gains.

For other mutual funds, income tax is payable on any dividends and gains made when the shares are sold. In addition, investors may also have to pay taxes each year on the fund's capital gains. This is because US law requires mutual funds to distribute capital gains to shareholders if they sell securities for a profit that cannot be offset by a loss.

The tax treatment of mutual funds for non-US residents means that, in practice, funds domiciled in Europe or elsewhere are more likely to be suitable.

2.2 European Open-Ended Funds

In Europe, three main types of funds are encountered – SICAVs, unit trusts and OEICs.

2.2.1 SICAVs and Fonds Commun de Placement (FCP)

As mentioned earlier, Luxembourg is one of the main centres for funds that are to be distributed to investors across European borders and globally. The main US fund groups along with their European counterparts manage huge fund ranges from Luxembourg, which are then distributed and sold not just across Europe but in the Middle East and Asia as well.

The main type of open-ended fund that is encountered is a **SICAV** – in other words, an open-ended investment company. Some of the main characteristics of SICAVs include:

- They are open-ended, so new shares can be created or shares can be cancelled to meet investor demand.
- Dealings are undertaken directly with the fund management group or through their network of agents.
- They are typically valued each day and the price at which shares are bought or sold is directly linked to the NAV of the underlying portfolio.
- They are **single-priced**, which means that the same price is used when buying or selling and any charges for purchases are added on afterwards.
- They are usually structured as an **umbrella fund**, which means that each fund will have multiple other funds sitting under one legal entity. This often means that switches from one fund to another can be made at a reduced charge or without any charge at all.

- Their legal structure is a **company** which is domiciled in Luxembourg and, although some of the key aspects of the administration of the fund must also be conducted there, the investment management is often undertaken in London or another European capital.

The other main type of structure encountered in Europe is an **FCP**. Like unit trusts (which are considered in more detail below), FCPs do not have a legal personality; instead, their structure is based on a contract between the scheme manager and the investors. The contract provides for the funds to be managed on a pooled basis.

As FCPs have no legal personality, they have to be administered by a management company, but otherwise the administration is very similar to that described above for SICAVs.

2.2.2 Unit Trusts

A unit trust is an investment fund that is established as a **trust**, in which the trustee is the legal owner of the underlying assets and the unit holders are the beneficial owners.

As with other types of OEICs, the trust can grow as more investors buy into the fund, or shrink as investors sell units back to the fund and they are cancelled. As with SICAVs, investors deal directly with the fund when they wish to buy and sell.

The major differences between unit trusts and the open-ended funds we have already looked at are the parties to the trust and how the units are priced.

The main parties to a unit trust are the unit trust manager and the trustee:

- The role of the **unit trust manager** is to decide, within the rules of the trust and the various regulations, which investments are included within the unit trust. This will include deciding what to buy and when to buy it, as well as what to sell and when to sell it. The unit trust manager may outsource this decision-making to a separate investment manager. The manager also provides a market for the units by dealing with investors who want to buy or sell units. It also carries out the daily pricing of units, based on the NAV of the underlying constituents.
- Every unit trust must also appoint a **trustee**. The trustee is the **legal owner** of the assets in the trust, holding the assets for the benefit of the underlying unit holders. The trustee also protects the interests of the investors by, among other things, monitoring the actions of the unit trust manager. Whenever new units are created for the trust, they are created by the trustee. The trustees are organisations that the unit holders can trust with their assets, normally large banks or insurance companies.

Just as with other investment funds, the price that an investor pays to buy a unit trust or receives when they sell is based on the NAV of the underlying portfolio. However, generally the pricing of units in a unit trust is done on a **dual-priced** basis rather than the single-priced basis adopted by SICAVs:

- The underlying portfolio of a unit trust is valued daily at both the bid and offer prices for the investments contained within the portfolio.
- This produces two NAVs, one representing the value at which the portfolio's investments can be sold for and another for how much it will cost to buy.

- These values are then used to calculate two separate prices, one at which investors can sell their units and one which the investor pays to buy units.

For this reason, unit trusts are described as **dual-priced**. They have a **bid price**, which is the price the investor receives if they are selling, and an **offer price**, which is the price the investor pays if buying. The difference between the two is known as the bid-offer spread.

Any initial charges made by the unit trust for buying the fund are included within the offer price that is quoted.

2.2.3 Open-Ended Investment Companies (OEICs)

An OEIC is another form of investment fund found in Europe. They are a form of **ICVC** that is structured as a company with the investors holding shares.

The term **'OEIC'** is used mostly in the UK, while in Ireland they are known as a **variable capital company (VCC)**. They have similar structures to SICAVs and, as with SICAVs and unit trusts, investors deal directly with the fund when they wish to buy and sell.

The key characteristics of OEICs are the parties that are involved and how they are priced.

- When an OEIC is set up, it is a requirement that an **authorised corporate director (ACD)** and a depository are appointed. The ACD is responsible for the day-to-day management of the fund, including managing the investments, valuing and pricing the fund and dealing with investors. It may undertake these activities itself or delegate them to specialist third parties.
- The fund's investments are held by an independent **depository**, responsible for looking after the investments on behalf of the fund's shareholders and overseeing the activities of the ACD. The depository plays a similar role to that of the trustee of a unit trust. The depository is the **legal owner** of the fund investments and the OEIC itself is the beneficial owner, not the shareholders.

The register of shareholders is maintained by the ACD.

An OEIC has the option to be either single-priced or dual-priced. In fact, most OEICs operate **single pricing**. Single pricing refers to the use of the mid-market prices of the underlying assets to produce a single price at which investors buy and sell. In other words, when a fund is single-priced, its underlying investments will be valued based on their mid-market value. This method of pricing does not provide the ability to recoup dealing expenses and commissions within the price. Such charges are instead separately identified for each transaction. It is important to note that the initial charge will be charged separately when comparing single-pricing to dual-pricing.

3. Closed-Ended Investment Companies

Learning Objective

7.3.1 Know the characteristics of closed-ended investment companies: share classes

7.3.2 Understand the factors that affect the price of closed-ended investment companies

7.3.3 Know the meaning of the discounts and premiums in relation to closed-ended investment companies

7.3.4 Know how closed-ended investment companies' shares are traded

A closed-ended investment company is another form of investment fund. When they are first established, a set number of shares is issued to the investing public, and these are then subsequently traded on a stock market. Investors wanting to subsequently buy shares do so on the stock market from investors who are willing to sell.

The capital of the fund is therefore fixed, and does not expand or contract in the way that an open-ended fund's capital does. For this reason, they are referred to as closed-ended funds in order to differentiate them from mutual funds, SICAVs, unit trusts and OEICs.

3.1 Characteristics of Closed-Ended Investment Companies

Closed-ended investment companies are found in both the US and Europe.

3.1.1 US

In the US, they are referred to as a **closed-end fund** and are one of the three basic types of investment companies alongside mutual funds (see Section 2.1) and unit investment trusts. In Europe, they are known as investment trusts or investment companies.

In the US, closed-end funds come in many varieties and can have different investment objectives, strategies and investment portfolios. They also can be subject to different risks, volatility and charges. They are permitted to invest in a greater amount of illiquid securities than are mutual funds. (An illiquid security generally is considered to be a security that cannot be sold within seven days at the approximate price used by the fund in determining NAV.) Because of this feature, funds that seek to invest in markets where the securities tend to be more illiquid are typically organised as closed-end funds.

The other main type of US investment company is a **unit investment trust (UIT)**. A UIT does not actively trade its investment portfolio, instead it buys a relatively fixed portfolio of securities – for example, five, ten or 20 specific stocks or bonds – and holds them with little or no change for the life of the fund.

Like a closed-end fund, it will usually make an initial public offering of its shares (or units), but the sponsors of the fund will maintain a secondary market, which allows owners of UIT units to sell them back to the sponsors and allows other investors to buy UIT units from the sponsors.

3.1.2 Europe

In Europe, closed-ended funds are usually known as **investment trusts** and more recently as **investment companies**.

Investment trusts were one of the first investment funds to be set up. The first funds were set up in the UK in the 1860s and, in fact, the very first investment trust to be established is still operating today. Its name is Foreign & Colonial Investment Trust, and it is a global growth trust that invests in over 30 markets and has around £2 billion of funds under management.

Despite its name, an investment trust is actually a **company**, not a trust. As a company it has directors and shareholders. However, like a unit trust, an investment trust will invest in a range of investments, allowing its shareholders to diversify and lessen their risk.

Some investment trust companies have more than one type of share. For example, an investment trust might issue both ordinary shares and preference shares. Such investment trusts are commonly referred to as **split capital investment trusts**.

In contrast with OEICs and unit trusts, investment trust companies are allowed to borrow money on a long-term basis by taking out bank loans and/or issuing bonds. This can enable them to invest the borrowed money in more stocks and shares – a process known as **gearing** or **leverage**.

Also, some investment trusts have a fixed date for their winding-up.

3.2 Pricing, Discounts and Premiums

The price of a share (except in the case of an OEIC, as we have seen) is what someone is prepared to pay for it. The price of a share in a closed-ended investment company is no different.

The share prices for closed-ended investment companies are therefore arrived at in a very different way from an open-ended fund.

Remember that units in a unit trust are bought and sold by their fund manager at a price that is based on the underlying value of the constituent investments. Shares in an OEIC are bought and sold by the ACD, again at the value of the underlying investments.

The share price of a closed-ended investment company, however, is not necessarily the same as the value of the underlying investments. It will value the underlying portfolio daily and provide details of the NAV to the stock exchange on which it is quoted and traded. The price it subsequently trades at, however, will be determined by demand and supply for the shares, and may be above or below the NAV.

When the share price is above the NAV, it is said to be **trading at a premium**. When the share price is below the NAV, it is said to be **trading at a discount**.

Example

ABC Investment Trust shares are trading at £2.30. The NAV per share is £2.00. ABC Investment Trust shares are trading at a premium. The premium is 15% of the underlying NAV.

Example

XYZ Investment Trust shares are trading at 95p. The NAV per share is £1.00. XYZ Investment Trust shares are trading at a discount. The discount is 5% of the underlying NAV.

Investment trust company shares generally trade at a discount to their NAV.

A number of factors contribute to the extent of the discount, and it will vary across different investment companies. Most importantly, the discount is a function of the market's view of the quality of the management of the investment trust portfolio and its choice of underlying investments. A smaller discount (or even a premium) will be displayed when investment trusts are nearing their winding-up, or about to undergo some corporate activity, such as a merger/takeover.

3.3 Trading in Investment Trust Company Shares

In the same way as other listed company shares, shares in investment trust companies are bought and sold on a stock exchange such as the NYSE or the LSE (London Stock Exchange).

3.4 Real Estate Investment Trusts (REITs)

Learning Objective

7.4.1 Know the basic characteristics of REITs: tax implications; property diversification; liquidity; risk

---

REITs are well established in countries such as the US, UK, Australia, Canada and France. Globally, the market is worth more than US$400 billion.

They are normal investment trust companies that pool investors' funds to invest in commercial and possibly residential property.

One of the main features of REITs is that they provide access to property returns without the previous disadvantage of double taxation. Until recently, when an investor held property company shares, not only would the company pay corporation tax, but the investor would be liable to tax on dividends and any growth. Under the rules for REITs, no corporation tax is payable, providing that certain conditions are met and distributions are instead taxable on the investor.

REITs give investors access to professional property investment and might provide them with new opportunities, such as the ability to invest in commercial property. This allows them to diversify the risk of holding direct property investments.

This type of investment trust also removes a further risk from holding direct property, namely liquidity risk or the risk that the investment will not be able to be readily realised. REITs are closed-ended funds and are quoted on stock exchanges, and shares in REITs are bought and sold in the same way as other investment trusts.

4. Exchange-Traded Funds (ETFs)

Learning Objective

7.5.1 Know the main characteristics of exchange-traded funds: trading; replication methods

An exchange-traded fund is an investment fund, usually designed to track a particular index. This is typically a stock market index, such as the S&P (Standard & Poor's) 500. The investor buys shares in the ETF which are **quoted on the stock exchange**, like investment trusts. However, unlike investment trusts, ETFs are **open-ended funds**. This means that, like OEICs, the fund gets bigger as more people invest and gets smaller as people withdraw their money.

ETF shares may trade at a premium or discount to the underlying investments, but the difference is minimal and the ETF share price essentially reflects the value of the investments in the fund. The investor's return is in the form of dividends paid by the ETF, and the possibility of a capital gain (or loss) on sale.

Shares in ETFs are bought and sold through a stockbroker on a stock exchange and exhibit the following charges:

- There is a spread between the price at which investors buy the shares and the price at which they can sell them. This is usually very small, for example just 0.1% or 0.2% for, say, an ETF tracking the FTSE 100.
- An annual management charge is deducted from the fund. Typically, this is 0.5% or less.
- The investors pay stockbroker's commission when they buy and sell. But, unlike other UK shares, there is no stamp duty to pay on purchases.

5. Hedge Funds

Learning Objective

7.6.1 Know the basic characteristics of hedge funds: risks; cost and liquidity; investment strategies

Hedge funds are reputed to be high-risk. However, in many cases, this perception stands at odds with reality. In their original incarnation, hedge funds sought to eliminate or reduce market risk. That said, there are now many different styles of hedge fund – some risk-averse, and some employing highly risky strategies. It is, therefore, not wise to generalise about them.

The most obvious market risk is the risk that is faced by an investor in shares – as the broad market moves down, the investor's shares also fall in value. Traditional 'absolute return' hedge funds attempt to profit regardless of the general movements of the market by carefully selecting a combination of asset classes, including derivatives, and by holding both long and short positions (a short position may involve the selling of shares which the fund does not at that time own in the hope of buying them back more cheaply if the market falls).

However, innovation has resulted in a wide range of complex hedge fund strategies, some of which place a greater emphasis on producing highly geared returns than on controlling market risk.

Many hedge funds have high initial investment levels, meaning that access is effectively restricted to wealthy investors and institutions.

The common aspects of hedge funds are the following:

- **Structure** – most hedge funds are established as unauthorised and therefore unregulated CISs, meaning that they cannot be generally marketed to private individuals because they are considered too risky for the less financially sophisticated investor.
- **High investment entry levels** – most hedge funds require minimum investments in excess of £50,000; some exceed £1 million.
- **Investment flexibility** – because of the lack of regulation, hedge funds are able to invest in whatever assets they wish (subject to compliance with the restrictions in their constitutional documents and prospectus). In addition to being able to take long and short positions in securities like shares and bonds, some take positions in commodities and currencies. Their investment style is generally aimed at producing absolute returns – positive returns regardless of the general direction of market movements.
- **Gearing** – many hedge funds can borrow funds and use derivatives to potentially enhance returns.
- **Liquidity** – to maximise the hedge fund manager's investment freedom, hedge funds usually impose an initial 'lock-in' period of between one and three months before investors can sell their investments on.
- **Cost** – hedge funds typically levy performance-related fees which the investor pays if certain performance levels are achieved, otherwise paying a fee comparable to that charged by other growth funds. Performance fees can be substantial, with 20% or more of the **net new highs** (also called the 'high water mark') being common.

6. Private Equity

Learning Objective

7.7.1 Know the basic characteristics of private equity: raising finance; realising capital gain

Private equity is medium- to long-term finance, provided in return for an equity stake in potentially high-growth companies. It can take many forms, from providing venture capital to complete buy-outs.

For a firm, attracting private equity investment is very different from raising a loan from a lender. Private equity is invested in exchange for a stake in a company and, as shareholders, the investors' returns are dependent on the growth and profitability of the business. They therefore face the risk of failure, just like the other shareholders.

The private equity firm is rewarded by the company's success, generally achieving its principal return through realising a capital gain on **exit**. This may involve:

- the private equity firm selling its shares back to the management of the investee company;
- the private equity firm selling the shares to another investor, such as another private equity firm;
- a trade sale, that is the sale of company shares to another firm; or
- the company achieving a stock market listing.

Private equity firms raise their capital from a variety of sources, but mainly from large investing institutions. These may be happy to entrust their money to the private equity firm because of its expertise in finding businesses with good potential.

Few people or institutions can afford the risk of investing directly in individual buy-outs and, instead, use pooled vehicles to achieve a diversification of risk. Traditionally this was through investment trusts, such as 3i or Electra Private Equity.

With the increasing amount of funds being raised for this asset class, methods of raising investment have moved on. Private equity arrangements are now usually structured in different ways from retail CISs. They are usually set up as limited partnerships with high minimum investment levels. Like hedge funds, there are generally restrictions on when an investor can realise their investment.

End of Chapter Questions

Think of an answer for each question and refer to the appropriate section for confirmation.

1. How might the pooling of investment aid a retail investor?
   Answer Reference: Section 1.1

2. What is an investment management approach that seeks to produce returns in line with an index known as?
   Answer Reference: Section 1.2

3. In which type of collective investment vehicle would you be most likely to expect to see a fund manager quote bid and offer prices?
   Answer Reference: Section 2.2.2

4. Who is the legal owner of the investments held in an OEIC?
   Answer Reference: Section 2.2.3

5. What are some of the principal ways in which investment trusts differ from authorised unit trusts and OEICs?
   Answer Reference: Section 3.1.2

6. How does the trading and settlement of an authorised unit trust differ from an ETF?
   Answer Reference: Sections 2.2.2 & 4

7. Which is an open-ended type of investment vehicle that is traded on a stock exchange?
   Answer Reference: Section 4

8. What type of investment vehicle makes extensive use of short positions?
   Answer Reference: Section 5

Chapter Eight

Regulation and Ethics

This syllabus area will provide approximately 5 of the 50 examination questions

1. Introduction

An understanding of regulation is essential in today's investment world. In this chapter, we will aim to take an overview of regulation by looking at it in an international context, before using the UK regime to consider some of the key principles of financial services regulation.

1.1 The Need for Regulation

Learning Objective

8.1.1 Understand the need for regulation

The risk of losing money that can arise from many types of financial transactions has meant that financial markets have always been subject to the need for rules and codes of conduct to protect investors and the general public, although these rules have not always been in place or enforced as robustly as they are today.

As markets developed, there grew a need for market participants to be able to set rules so that there were agreed standards of behaviour and to provide a mechanism so that disputes could be settled readily. This need developed into what is known as self-regulation, when, for example, as well as fulfilling its main function of providing a secondary market for shares, a stock exchange would also set rules for its members and police their implementation.

With the development of global financial markets came the need for improved and common standards, as well as international co-operation. Self-regulation became increasingly untenable and most countries moved to a statutory approach (that is, with rules laid down by law so that breaking them is a criminal offence). They also established their own, independent regulatory bodies. The need for international co-operation between regulatory bodies also led to the creation of an international organisation, the International Organization of Securities Commissions (**IOSCO**).

IOSCO designs objectives and standards that are used by the world's regulators as international benchmarks for all securities markets. These objectives and standards can be seen in most systems of securities regulation. Today there is a significant level of co-operation between financial services regulators worldwide and, increasingly, they are imposing common standards. Anti-money laundering rules are probably the best example.

The advantage of a common set of rules can also be seen in the rationale behind **EU directives**. As well as aiming to ensure that it has world class regulatory standards, the EU is also particularly concerned with the development of a single market in financial services across Europe. This has been a major feature of European financial services legislation for some time and brings in standards that are designed to ensure that each country in Europe operates under the same detailed regulatory regime.

Regulation is still developing. The financial turmoil seen in markets recently has raised the need for more regulation and highlighted the importance of a globally co-ordinated approach. Radical changes in this area are now being implemented by international bodies and regulators worldwide.

1.2 Regulatory Principles

Learning Objective

8.1.2 Understand the main aims and activities of financial services regulators

Governments are responsible for setting the role of regulators and in so doing will clearly look to see that international best practice is adopted through the implementation of IOSCO objectives and principles and by co-operation with other international regulators and supervisors.

As an example of this, European governments co-operate regionally to ensure there is a framework of regulation that encourages the cross-border provision of financial services across Europe by standardising or harmonising each country's respective approach. European regulators co-operate to co-ordinate activities and draft the detailed rules needed to introduce pan-European regulation through the **European Securities and Markets Authority (ESMA)**.

In Asia, the basic structure and content of securities regulation is increasingly similar to the model adopted in most other parts of the world. Most countries are members of IOSCO and subscribe to its principles of securities regulation. It is similar in the Middle East where regulators have looked to take examples of best regulatory practice from countries such as the UK and Australia and have then adapted them to their local markets.

Regulators will typically be given a set of objectives by governments. A summarised example of these from a variety of regulators is shown in the table on the following page. The main purposes and aims of regulation, in all markets globally, are to:

- maintain and promote fairness, efficiency, competitiveness, transparency and orderliness;
- promote understanding by the public of the operation and functioning of the financial services industry;
- provide protection for members of the public investing in or holding financial products;
- minimise crime and misconduct in the industry;
- reduce systemic risks; and
- assist in maintaining the market's financial stability by taking appropriate steps.

In order to achieve the main objectives of financial regulation, regulators worldwide have developed a series of codes of conduct that are used to set standards for businesses and individuals. Later, in Section 4, we will consider the Code of Conduct issued by the Chartered Institute for Securities & Investment (CISI) as an example of how professional bodies also have a role to play in setting acceptable standards of behaviour.

US – Securities and Exchange Commission (SEC)	UK – Prudential Regulation Authority (PRA) and Financial Conduct Authority (FCA)	Dubai Financial Services Authority (DFSA)	Chinese Securities Regulatory Commission (CSRC)
Foster and enforce compliance with the federal securities laws	Promote the safety and soundness of firms, focusing on the harm that firms can cause to the stability of the financial system	Maintain fairness, transparency and efficiency	Supervision of securities and futures markets
Establish an effective regulatory environment	Secure an appropriate degree of protection for consumers	Maintain confidence in financial industry	Increase ability to handle and prevent financial crises
Facilitate access to the information investors need to make informed investment decisions	Promote efficiency and choice in the market for financial services	Maintain financial stability and reduce systemic risk	Prepare regulations for securities markets
Enhance SEC performance through effective alignment and management of human, information, and financial capital	Protect and enhance the integrity of the financial system	Prevent conduct that damages the financial services industry	Exercise supervision of securities businesses
		Promote public understanding and protect users of financial services	Investigate and penalise violations of securities laws

2. Money Laundering

Money laundering is the process of turning money that is derived from criminal activities – **dirty money** – into money which appears to have been legitimately acquired and which can therefore be more easily invested and spent – **clean money**.

Money laundering can take many forms, including:

- turning money acquired through criminal activity into clean money;
- handling the proceeds of crimes such as theft, fraud and tax evasion;
- handling stolen goods;
- being directly involved with, or facilitating, the laundering of any criminal or terrorist property;
- criminals investing the proceeds of their crimes in the whole range of financial products.

There can be considerable similarities between the movement of terrorist funds and the laundering of criminal property and, because terrorist groups can have links with other criminal activities, there is inevitably some overlap between anti-money laundering provisions and the rules designed to prevent the financing of terrorist acts. There are two major differences to note, however, between terrorist financing and other money laundering activities:

- Often, only quite small sums of money are required to commit terrorist acts, making identification and tracking more difficult.
- If legitimate funds are used to fund terrorist activities, it is difficult to identify when the funds become terrorist funds.

Terrorist organisations can, however, require significant funding and will employ modern techniques to manage the funds and transfer them between jurisdictions, hence the similarities with money laundering. The cross-border nature of money laundering and terrorist financing has led to international co-ordination to ensure that countries have legislation and regulatory processes in place to enable identification and prosecution of those involved.

Examples include:

- The **Financial Action Task Force (FATF)**, which has issued recommendations aimed at setting minimum standards for action in different countries to ensure anti-money laundering efforts are consistent internationally. It has also issued special recommendations on terrorist financing.
- **EU directives** targeted at money laundering prevention.
- **Standards issued by international bodies** to encourage due diligence procedures to be followed for customer identification.
- Sanctions by the **United Nations (UN)** and the **EU** to deny access to the financial services sector to individuals and organisations from certain countries.
- Guidance issued by the private sector **Wolfsberg Group** of banks in relation to private banking, correspondent banking and other activities.

2.1 Stages of Money Laundering

Learning Objective

8.2.1 Understand the terms that describe the three main stages of money laundering

---

There are three stages to a successful money laundering operation:

- **Placement** is the first stage and typically involves placing the criminally derived cash into an account with a bank or other financial institution.
- **Layering** is the second stage and involves moving the money around in order to make it difficult for the authorities to link the placed funds with the ultimate beneficiary of the money. Disguising the original source of the funds might involve buying and selling foreign currencies, shares or bonds.
- **Integration** is the third and final stage. At this stage, the layering has been successful and the ultimate beneficiary appears to be holding legitimate funds (clean money rather than dirty money). The money is integrated back into the financial system and dealt with as if it were legitimate.

Broadly, the anti-money laundering provisions are aimed at identifying suspicious activity, including through familiarity with customers, and through reporting suspicions at the placement and layering stages.

In addition, firms are required to keep adequate records so that an audit trail can be established if the need arises.

2.2 Reporting to the Authorities

Learning Objective

8.2.2 Know the action to be taken by those employed in financial services if money laundering activity is suspected

Regulations surrounding financial crime make it an offence to fail to disclose a suspicion of money laundering. Obviously this requires staff in financial services firms to be aware of what should arouse their suspicion, and this is why there is a requirement that staff must be trained to recognise and deal with what may be money laundering transactions.

The disclosure of suspicions is ultimately made to the legal authorities. However, disclosure goes through two stages. First, a suspicion is disclosed within the firm to a person who is appointed as the money laundering reporting officer (MLRO). It is the MLRO who decides whether the suspicion that has been reported to him is sufficient to pass on. If so, he will pass it to the appropriate authorities.

It is important to appreciate that by reporting to the MLRO, the employee with the suspicion has fulfilled his responsibilities under the law – he has disclosed his suspicions.

Similarly, by reporting to the authorities, the MLRO has fulfilled his responsibilities under the law.

3. Insider Trading and Market Abuse

3.1 Insider Trading

Learning Objective

8.3.1 Know the offences that constitute insider trading and the instruments covered

When directors or employees of a listed company buy or sell shares in that company, there is a possibility that they are committing a criminal act – insider dealing.

For example, a director may be buying shares in the knowledge that the company's last six months of trade was better than the market expected. The director has the benefit of this information because he is 'inside' the company. In nearly all markets, this would be a criminal offence, punishable by a fine and/or a jail term.

To find someone guilty of insider dealing it is necessary to define who is deemed to be an insider, what is deemed to be inside information and the situations that give rise to the offence.

Inside information is information that relates to particular securities or a particular issuer of securities (and not to securities or securities issuers generally) and:

- is specific or precise;
- has not been made public; and
- if it were made public, would be likely to have a significant effect on the price of the securities.

This is generally referred to as **unpublished price-sensitive information**, and the securities are referred to as **price-affected securities**. The information becomes public when it is published.

Information can be treated as public even though it may be acquired by persons only exercising diligence or expertise (for example, by careful analysis of published accounts, or by scouring a library).

A person has price-sensitive information as an **insider** if he knows that it is inside information from an inside source. The person may have:

1. gained the information through being a director, employee or shareholder of an issuer of securities;
2. gained access to the information by virtue of his employment, office or profession (for example, the auditors to the company);
3. sourced the information from (1) or (2), either directly or indirectly.

Insider trading takes place when an insider acquires, or disposes of, price-affected securities while in possession of unpublished price-sensitive information. It also occurs if they encourage another person to deal in price-affected securities, or to disclose the information to another person (other than in the proper performance of employment).

The instruments covered by the insider trading rules are usually broadly described as 'securities', which include:

- shares;
- bonds (issued by a company or a public sector body);
- warrants;
- depositary receipts;
- options (to acquire or dispose of securities);
- futures (to acquire or dispose of securities);
- contracts for difference (based on securities, interest rates or share indices).

Note that the definition of securities does not embrace commodities and derivatives on commodities (such as options and futures on agricultural products, metals or energy products), or units/shares in open-ended collective investment schemes.

3.2 Market Abuse

Learning Objective

8.3.2 Know the offences that constitute market abuse and the instruments covered

Market abuse relates to behaviour by a person or a group of people working together and which satisfies one or more of the following three conditions:

- The behaviour is based on information that is not generally available to those using the market and which, if it were available, would have an impact on the price.
- The behaviour is likely to give a false or misleading impression of the supply, demand or value of the investments concerned.
- The behaviour is likely to distort the market in the investments.

In all three cases the behaviour is judged on the basis of what a **regular user** of the market would view as a failure to observe the standards of behaviour normally expected in the market.

An example of prohibited **market abuse** was the spreading of false rumours in March 2008 about certain companies listed on the London Stock Exchange (LSE). It was suspected that those spreading the rumours were holding short positions in the companies – in other words, they had sold shares which they did not own, in the hope of buying them back at a lower price in the future. The spreading of false rumours was designed to push down the price.

Market abuse does not have the same restrictions on the instruments covered as the insider trading regime. Broadly, market abuse covers financial instruments that are traded on exchanges, which includes not only shares and bonds and related derivatives, but also commodity derivatives.

4. Integrity and Ethics in Professional Practice

Learning Objective

8.1.4 Understand the key principles of professional integrity and ethical behaviour in financial services

We are all faced with ethical choices on a regular basis, and doing the right thing is usually obvious. Yet there have been many situations in the news recently in which seemingly rational people have behaved unethically. Is this because they consider that there are some situations when ethics apply and others when they do not? Is it because they did not think that their behaviour was unethical? Or maybe it was just that they thought they could get away with it? Or could it be that, in actual fact, it involves all of these thoughts and actions and some more besides?

Despite the relationship between the two, ethics should not be seen as a subset of regulation, but as an important topic in its own right.

4.1 Ethical or Unethical Practice?

One of the observations sometimes made about ethics is that the benefit of ignoring ethical standards and behaviour far outweighs the benefit of adhering to them, both from an individual and also a corporate perspective.

What this argument ignores is that, while such a policy may make sense and be sustainable for a short period, in our society the inevitable outcome is likely to be at least social and at worst criminal sanctions.

An obvious example is the selling of products that carry a high level of commission for the salesman. Although there may be benefits to all three parties to the transaction – the product provider (originator), the intermediary (salesman) and the purchaser (customer) – the structure of the process contains a salient feature (high commission) which has the capability to skew the process.

It can be argued that there is nothing wrong with such a structure, which simply reflects an established method of doing business around the world. However, there are fundamental differences in the financial services industry which could affect the relationship between the salesman and the customer. If you buy a car, you can see it, you can try it out and you will discover very quickly whether it performs in the manner advertised and which you expect. You will also be provided, in the case of a new car, with a warranty from the manufacturer. You can thus make your purchase decision with considerable confidence, despite knowing that the reward system in the motor industry means that the salesman will almost certainly receive a commission.

Contrast this with an imaginary financial product. This may be an arena in which you are less than knowledgeable, and the product may be one to which, once committed, you can have no idea about its quality for many years to come, by which time it may be too late to make changes or seek redress.

An ethical salesman should therefore take you through the structure of, say, a long-term investment instrument in such a manner that you may be reasonably assured that you understand what it is and from whom you are buying the product. They should explain the factors which determine the rate of return that is offered, and tell you whether that is an actual rate, or an anticipated rate which is dependent upon certain other things happening, over which the product originator may have no control. They should also tell you what they are being paid if you buy the product.

In other words they will give you all the facts that you need to make an informed decision as to whether you wish to invest. They will be **OPEN, HONEST, TRANSPARENT and FAIR**.

4.2 An Ethical Corporate Culture

Stephen Green, group chairman of HSBC, said: *'Part of the responsibility of top management is to ensure that the culture of the organisation reinforces the ethical behaviour that is a prerequisite of our industry. The example set by the people at the top will always have a huge influence on how the rest of the organisation behaves.'*

'Culture' can be described but not easily defined. Nor can it be imposed by just putting in a programme. It must be recognised by those inside who are employed, and by those outside who come into contact with the business.

At its most basic, corporate culture expresses itself in behaviour and the way a business is run. Staff are sensitive to management style. When faced with a business problem, a manager has to balance the legitimate requirements of attaining business objectives and the ethical requirements of honesty and integrity in the way this is achieved. If staff see from their managers' decisions that the prevailing culture is one of trust, integrity and openness, they generally will feel comfortable at work and be proud of the organisation. And this is likely to be reflected in their own dealings with others.

For an ethical culture to be successful, it must have regard to all of those people and organisations who are affected by it.

The principal constituents of an organisation and its financial relationships are summarised in the following table. These are all the people, groups and interests with whom a business has a relationship and who will, therefore, be affected by its fundamental ethical values.

Stakeholder	Financial Relationship
Shareholder	Dividends and asset value growth
Provider of finance (lender)	Interest and capital repayments
Employee	Wages, salary, pensions, bonus, other financial benefits
Customer	Payments for goods and services (receipts)
Suppliers	Payments for goods and services (invoices)
Community	Taxes and excise duties, licence fees

Example

A builder (supplier) offers a customer an apparent incentive: the frequently seen 'discount for cash payment'. But what is his primary motivation? While it may be to give the customer a good deal and so to win the business for himself, this is being achieved through the likely under-reporting of his income and thus under-collection of legitimate taxes, both income and VAT.

So what would you do? Would you insist that you will make payment only against a proper invoice, knowing that you will also have to pay value added tax (VAT)? Or would you be willing to compromise your ethical standards, using the argument that what you are doing 'goes on all the time'?

Would you do that on a business contract at work? Does your company policy allow it? Almost certainly not.

This is a simple example, but in the business context there are numerous other interests to be taken into account when considering who will be affected and in what way. This starts with the smallest participant – you as an individual – and can be followed through to affect all of the stakeholders in the business.

Your actions will affect your team, which may be defined as any colleagues with whom you work, up to the whole business itself, depending upon its size. The business will have shareholders and, as a result of your actions improving the profitability of the business, a dividend may be paid that otherwise would not have been paid. So your action will have impacted them, apparently positively. Had you asked them whether they supported your activities, however, knowing what was involved, is it likely that they would have agreed?

And what about the impact upon your external stakeholders: other suppliers and customers who become aware of the standards which your firm has adopted? Are they likely to be reassured?

So what may start out as a well-intentioned but inadequately thought-out action may have consequences which extend far beyond your immediate area.

4.3 The Positive Effects of Ethical Approaches on Corporate Sustainability

Regrettably, we are only too familiar with examples of unethical behaviour having a terminal impact on business, with the names of Enron, Tyco, Worldcom and Parmalat springing readily to mind. Equally, the generally low public regard in which the banking industry is held, as a result of what are perceived to be unethical remuneration practices, provides another salutary example.

One reason for the poor regard that people have for business people and their integrity is that business leaders rarely discuss business values and ethics in public or even in private. As a result, there tends to be reluctance among employees to question decisions of management or raise concerns.

The reticence of leaders to speak up about standards in commercial life may be partly due to uncertainty about the business case for insisting on high ethical standards in business. If a link could be established, therefore, between always doing business responsibly and consistently good financial performance, then there would be more reason for directors of companies to speak up about, and insist on, high ethical standards in their organisations. This includes policy and strategy decisions in the boardroom, and integrity throughout their organisations.

And it is feasible to make such a link.

Research[1] shows more business leaders now understand that the way they do business is an important aspect of fulfilling their financial obligations to their stockholders, as well as other stakeholders. They are responding to accusations of poor behavioural standards in various ways.

First, more companies are putting in place corporate responsibility policies or ethics policies, the principal feature of which is a code of ethics/conduct/behaviour to guide the staff. Companies now accept that an ethics policy is one of the essential ingredients of good corporate governance.

Second, modern corporate governance procedures include risk assessments, and until recently these tended to be confined to the financial, legal and safety hazards of the organisation, but growing numbers of companies are recognising reputation and branding issues around lack of integrity as a possible source of future problems. For example, Royal Dutch Shell identifies this among its risk factors

1 Webley, S. and Werner, A., '*Employee Views of Ethics at Work*', Institute of Business Ethics, 2009.

in its 2008 Annual Review: *'An erosion of Shell's business reputation would adversely impact our licence to operate, our brand, our ability to secure new resources and our financial performance.'*

But can the time and effort put into designing and implementing such guidance, including a code of conduct/ethics/practice, be shown to make a difference? Does doing business ethically pay?

Recent studies have provided a positive answer to this question. In 2002–03 the Institute of Business Ethics (IBE) undertook research showing that, for large UK companies, having an ethics policy (a code) operating for at least five years correlated with above-average financial performance based on four measures of value. The performance of a control cohort of similar companies without an explicit ethics policy – no code – was used for comparison. This was published by IBE in April 2003 under the title *'Does Business Ethics Pay?'*[2] The methodology developed for this project was used in a more recent study by researchers at Cranfield University and the IBE using more up-to-date data. They came to a similar conclusion.[3]

So what makes the difference? A pilot study to the Cranfield/IBE report investigated the distinguishing features, if any, of the operations of companies with explicit ethics policies compared with those with a less robust policy.

Employee Retention

One non-financial indicator is the retention of high-quality staff, recognised as vital to a profitable and sustainable organisation. The attraction and retention of high quality staff would be expected to be reflected in higher productivity and, ultimately, profitability. This is well explained in *'Putting the Service-Profit Chain to Work'*,[4] in which the authors describe the links in the service-profit chain. They argue that profit and growth are stimulated by customer loyalty; loyalty is a direct result of customer satisfaction; satisfaction is largely influenced by the value of services provided to customers; value is created by satisfied, loyal and productive employees; and employee satisfaction, in turn, results from high-quality support services and policies that enable employees to deliver results to customers.

Customer Retention

A second non-financial indicator is customer retention. It, too, is recognised as a significant factor in the long-term viability of a company. A research paper in 2002[5] showed that corporate ethical character makes a difference to the way that customers (and other stakeholders) identify with the company (brand awareness).

Besides maintaining good staff and customers, how providers of finance and insurance rate an organisation is a major factor in determining the cost of each. What ratings agencies have developed, with varying degrees of success, are measures of risk – the lower the risk, the lower the capital cost. One study, using Standard and Poor's and Barclays Bank data, has indicated that companies with an

2 Webley, S. and More, E., *'Does Business Ethics Pay? Ethics and Financial Performance'*, Institute of Business Ethics, 2003.

3 Ugoji, K., Dando, N. and Moir, L., *'Does Business Ethics Pay? Revisited: The Value of Ethics Training'*, Institute of Business Ethics, 2007.

4 *'Putting the Service Profit Chain to Work'*, HBR, July/August 2008.

5 Chun, R., *'An Alternative Approach to Appraising Corporate Social Performance: Stakeholder Emotion'*, Manchester Business School. Submitted to Academy of Management Conference, Denver, Colorado, 2002.

explicit ethics policy generally have a higher rating than those without one. This in turn generated a significantly lower cost of capital.[6]

What is apparent from these research projects, and others in the US, is that the leadership of consistently well-managed companies accepts that having a corporate responsibility/ethics policy is an important part of their corporate governance agenda.

4.4 Assessing Dilemmas

Many firms and individuals maintain the highest standards without feeling the need for a plethora of formal policies and procedures documenting conformity with accepted ethical standards. Nevertheless, it cannot be assumed that ethical awareness will be absorbed through a sort of process of osmosis. Accordingly, if we are to achieve the highest standards of ethical behaviour in our industry, and in industry more generally, it is sensible to consider how we can create a sense of ethical awareness.

If we accept that ethics is about both thinking and doing the right thing, then we should seek first of all to instil the type of thinking which causes us, as a matter of habit, to reflect upon what we are considering doing, or what we may be asked to do, before we carry it out.

There will often be situations, particularly at work, when we are faced with a decision, when it is not immediately obvious whether what we are being asked to do is actually right.

A simple checklist will help to decide. Is it:

- **Open** – is everyone whom your action or decision affects fully aware of it, or will they be made aware of it?
- **Honest** – does it comply with applicable law or regulation?
- **Transparent** – is it clear to all parties involved what is happening/will happen?
- **Fair** – is the transaction or decision fair to everyone involved in it or affected by it?

A simple and often quoted test is whether you would be happy to appear in the media in connection with, or in justification of, the transaction or decision.

4.5 Codes of Ethics, Codes of Conduct, and Regulation

For any industry in which trust is a central feature, demonstrable standards of practice and the means to enforce them are a key requirement. Hence the proliferation of professional bodies in the fields of health and wealth – areas in which consumers are more sensitive to performance and have higher expectations than in many other fields.

It should be noted that, although the terms 'code of ethics' and 'code of conduct' are often used synonymously, using the term 'ethics' to describe the nature of a code whose purpose is to establish standards of behaviour does, undoubtedly, imply that it involves commitment to and conformity with standards of personal morality, rather than simply complying with rules and guidance relating to professional dealings. Such instructions may be contained more appropriately within a document

6 Webley, S. and Hamilton, K., *'How Does Business Ethics Pay?'* in Appendix 3 of *'Does Business Ethics Pay? Revisited'*, 2007, op.cit.

described as a **code of conduct**. If it is considered that more specific guidance of standards of professional practice would be beneficial, such standards might be set out in an appropriately entitled document, or in **regulatory standards**.

Within financial services we have a structure where, in most countries, detailed and prescriptive regulation is imposed by regulatory bodies (see Section 1.2). In the UK, until 31 March 2013 this body was the Financial Services Authority (FSA) which, when initially established, other than through the high-level medium of the Principles for Businesses and Principles for Approved Persons, did not impose any stated standards of ethical behaviour.

Nevertheless, professional bodies operating in the field of financial services have developed codes of conduct for their members, and the following chart indicates the areas of responsibility that a sample of these cover.

Body	Society	Client	Employer	Professional Association	Profession	Colleagues/ Employer	Self	Others
A	✓	✓	✓	✓	✓	✓	✓	✓
B		✓	✓		✓	✓	✓	✓
C		✓		✓	✓		✓	✓
D	✓	✓	✓	✓	✓	✓	✓	✓
E		✓	✓	✓	✓	✓	✓	✓
F	✓	✓		✓	✓	✓	✓	
G	✓	✓		✓	✓		✓	✓
H		✓	✓	✓	✓		✓	✓
I	✓	✓			✓			✓

It is apparent from this chart that there are only two areas, 'responsibility to the client' and 'responsibility to the profession', which all the sampled codes of professional bodies have in common. This falls short of the aim of regulatory standards, which by their very nature must apply to everyone.

Consequently, while regulatory standards may *draw on* professional codes of conduct, they will not simply mirror them. However, the overarching connection between all three of these areas is an explicit requirement for the highest standards of personal and professional ethics.

One of the paradoxical outcomes of the financial crisis is that rule-based compliance is being strengthened, as it is judged that reliance upon principles-based decision-making is deemed to have failed. However, while this may be a natural reaction, the strengthening of regulation, far from being an indication of the failure or weakness of an ethically based approach, should in fact be seen as a clarion call for the strengthening of ethical standards.

These are the principal features of what we can describe as the 'ethics versus compliance' approach:

Ethics	Compliance
Prevention	Detection
Principles-based	Law/rules-based
Values-driven	Fear-driven
Implicit	Explicit
Spirit of the law	Letter of the law
Discretionary	Mandatory

Once again it is back to the choice of doing things because you *ought* to, it is the right thing to do, (ethics) rather than because you *have* to (rules).

4.5.1 UK Regulatory Principles

From the outset of its role as the sole regulator for the UK financial services industry on 1 December 2001, the FSA operated without a formal code of ethics, since the original view was that establishing ethical standards and the policing of ethical behaviour was not an appropriate responsibility for a regulator.

However, as outlined in Sections 1.2.1 and 1.2.2, there were principles established both for FSA-regulated business itself and also for approved persons, and both sets of principles were capable of being invoked when considering the behaviour of industry participants that, while not being breaches of actual regulation, were considered to be inappropriate or damaging to the industry.

It is worth noting that the key verb in both sets of principles is the word '**must**', a command verb indicating that the subject has no discretion in what decision they make, because the Principle determines the correct course of action.

Events since 2001 caused the UK regulator to revise its belief in the adequacy of the approach that combines regulation with principles, since it is felt that this results in an overly black and white approach, ie, if an action is not specifically prevented by the regulations or Principles then it is acceptable to follow that course of action. Such an approach is popular in a number of countries, but is now felt to fall short of what is required in order to produce properly balanced decisions and policies.

4.5.2 CISI Code of Conduct

Learning Objective

8.1.3 Know the CISI Code of Conduct

For any industry in which trust is a central feature, demonstrable standards of practice and the means to enforce them are a key requirement.

Financial services is one such industry, and the CISI already has in place its own code of conduct. Membership of the Chartered Institute for Securities & Investment (the CISI) requires members to meet the standards set out within the Institute's principles.

These words are from the introduction:

'Professionals within the securities and investment industry owe important duties to their clients, the market, the industry and society at large. Where these duties are set out in law, or in regulation, the professional must always comply with the requirements in an open and transparent manner.

Membership of the Chartered Institute for Securities & Investment requires members to meet the standards set out within the Institute's Principles. These Principles impose an obligation on members to act in a way beyond mere compliance.'

They set out clearly the expectations upon members of the industry *'to act in a way beyond mere compliance'*. In other words, we must understand the obligation upon us to act with integrity in all aspects of our work and our professional relationships.

Accordingly, it is appropriate at this stage to examine the Code of Conduct and to remind ourselves of the stakeholders in each of the individual principles.

	The Principles	Stakeholder
1.	To act honestly and fairly at all times when dealing with clients, customers and counterparties and to be a good steward of their interests, taking into account the nature of the business relationship with each of them, the nature of the service to be provided to them and the individual mandates given by them.	Client
2.	To act with integrity in fulfilling the responsibilities of your appointment and to seek to avoid any acts, omissions or business practices which damage the reputation of your organisation or the financial services industry.	Firm/industry
3.	To observe applicable law, regulations and professional conduct standards when carrying out financial service activities, and to interpret and apply them to the best of your ability according to principles rooted in trust, honesty and integrity.	Regulator

4.	To observe the standards of market integrity, good practice and conduct required or expected of participants in markets when engaging in any form of market dealing.	Market participant
5.	To be alert to and manage fairly and effectively and to the best of your ability any relevant conflict of interest.	Client
6.	To attain and actively manage a level of professional competence appropriate to your responsibilities, to commit to continuing learning to ensure the currency of your knowledge, skills and expertise and to promote the development of others.	Client Colleagues Self
7.	To decline to act in any matter about which you are not competent unless you have access to such advice and assistance as will enable you to carry out the work in a professional manner.	Client
8.	To strive to uphold the highest personal and professional standards.	Industry Self

The Code of Conduct is intended to provide direction to members of the CISI.

At the corporate and institutional level, this means operating in accordance with the rules of market conduct, dealing fairly (honestly) with other market participants and not seeking to take unfair advantage of either. That does not mean that firms cannot be competitive, but that rules and standards of behaviour are required to enable markets to function smoothly, on top of the actual regulations which provide direction for the technical elements of market operation. At the individual client relationship level, the Code highlights the ethical responsibilities towards clients, over and above complying with the regulatory framework and our legal responsibilities.

But, as we have been discussing throughout this section, if you are guided by ethical principles, compliance with regulation is made very much easier!

At the conclusion of this section, let us consider the words of Guy Jubb, investment director and head of corporate governance at Standard Life, when speaking at the CISI annual ethics debate (2009).

'It's personal, we as individuals are the City. We must take our responsibility for restoring trust and there can be no abdication of responsibility to third parties; we must conduct our affairs as good stewards; we must sort out right from wrong and behave accordingly... members must live out being good stewards in the interests of their clients.'

End of Chapter Questions

Think of an answer for each question and refer to the appropriate section for confirmation.

1. What was IOSCO set up to facilitate?
   Answer Reference: Section 1.1

2. List three common aims of financial services regulators globally.
   Answer Reference: Section 1.2

3. What are the three stages of money laundering?
   Answer Reference: Section 2.1

4. What is meant by the term 'inside information'?
   Answer Reference: Section 3.1

5. What types of securities do the insider dealing rules apply to?
   Answer Reference: Section 3.1

6. What types of behaviour might lead to a charge of market abuse?
   Answer Reference: Section 3.2

Chapter Nine

Other Financial Products

This syllabus area will provide approximately 6 of the 50 examination questions

9

1. Pensions

Learning Objective

9.1.1 Know the reasons for retirement planning

9.1.2 Know the basic features and risk characteristics of retirement funds: state schemes; corporate retirement plans (defined benefit; defined contribution); personal schemes

1.1 Retirement Planning

For many people, their retirement fund and their home represent their main assets.

A pension is an investment fund where contributions are made, usually throughout the individual's working life, to provide a lump sum on retirement plus an annual pension payable thereafter. In many countries, pension contributions are generally tax-efficient – they reduce the amount of an individual's taxable income and, therefore, the amount of income tax paid. These tax advantages are put in place by the government to encourage people to provide for their old age. The pensions themselves tend to be subject to income tax when they are received.

1.2 State Pension Schemes

A state pension is provided in many countries to provide people in retirement with the funds to live.

The provision will obviously vary from country to country, but one of the common features in many countries is that state pensions are provided out of a government's current year income, with no investment for future needs.

This is a problem in many countries since people are living longer in retirement, and so present serious funding issues for governments. In the UK, for example, dependency ratios (the proportion of working people to retired people) are forecast to be 3:1 by 2030 and 2.5:1 by 2050. This means that by 2050, either each worker will have to support almost twice as many retired people, or support per head will need to fall substantially, or some combination of these changes.

Developing economies, such as India, have relatively low dependency ratios due to their relatively young populations. The challenge instead will be how to create an inclusive, affordable and fair pension system and how people provide for retirement in future as wealth and living standards improve.

1.3 Corporate Retirement Schemes

One of the earliest kinds of scheme supplementing state funding was the occupational pension scheme. Corporate retirement schemes or occupational pension schemes are run by companies for their employees.

The advantages of these schemes are:

- Employers contribute to the fund (some pension schemes do not involve any contributions from the employee – these are called non-contributory schemes).
- Running costs are often lower than for personal schemes and the costs are often met by the employer.
- The employer must ensure the fund is well run and for defined benefit schemes must make up any shortfall in funding.

In an occupational pension scheme, the employer makes pension contributions on behalf of its workers. For example, an occupational pension scheme might provide an employee with 1/40th of their final salary for every year of service. The employee could then retire with an annual pension the size of which was related to the number of years' service and the salary earned. This type of occupational pension scheme is known as a **final salary scheme** or **defined benefit scheme**. Many private sector employers have stopped providing such occupational schemes to new employees because of rising life expectancies and volatile investment returns, and the implications these factors have on the funding requirement for defined benefit schemes.

Instead, occupational pension schemes are now typically provided to new employees on a **defined contribution** basis – where the size of the pension is driven by the contributions paid and the investment performance of the fund. Under this type of scheme, an investment fund is built up and the amount of pension that will be received at retirement will be determined by the value of the fund and the amount of pension it can generate.

The higher cost of providing a defined benefit scheme is part of the reason why many companies have closed their defined benefit schemes to new joiners and make only defined contribution schemes available to staff. A key advantage of defined contribution schemes for employers over defined benefit schemes is that poor performance is not the employer's problem; it is the employee who will end up with a smaller pension.

Occupational pension schemes are generally structured as trusts, with the investment portfolio managed by professional asset managers. The asset managers are appointed by, and report to, the trustees of the scheme. The trustees will, typically, include representatives from the company (eg, company directors), as well as employee representatives.

1.4 Personal Pensions

Private pensions or personal pensions are individual pension plans. They are defined contribution schemes that might be used by employees of companies that do not run their own scheme, or where employees opt out of the company scheme, or they might be used in addition to an existing pension scheme, and by the self-employed.

Many employers actually organise personal pension schemes for their employees by arranging the administration of these schemes with an insurance company or an asset management firm. Such employers may also contribute to the personal pension schemes of their employees.

Employees and the self-employed who wish to provide for their pension and do not have access to occupational schemes or employer-arranged personal pensions have to organise their own personal pension schemes. These will often be arranged through an insurance company or an asset manager, where the individual can choose from the variety of investment funds offered.

In a private scheme, the key responsibility that lies with the individual is that the individual chooses the investment fund or direct holdings in a scheme administered by an insurance company or asset manager. It is then up to the individual to monitor the performance of their investments and assess whether it will be sufficient for their retirement needs.

1.4.1 Individual Retirement Accounts

Individual retirement accounts (IRAs) are found only in the US and are effectively a type of personal pension scheme. They are established by individual taxpayers and contributions can be made up to a maximum amount which can qualify for tax deduction. Contributions to a traditional IRA may be tax-deductible depending on the taxpayer's income, tax filing status and coverage by an employer-sponsored retirement plan.

2. Loans

Learning Objective

9.2.1 Know the differences between bank loans, overdrafts and credit card borrowing

9.2.4 Know the difference between secured and unsecured borrowing

2.1 Types of Borrowing

Individuals can borrow money from banks and other financial institutions in three main ways:

- overdrafts;
- credit card borrowing; and
- loans.

2.1.1 Overdrafts

When an individual draws out more money than he holds in his bank account, he becomes overdrawn. His account is described as being in overdraft.

If the amount overdrawn is within a limit previously agreed with the bank, the overdraft is said to be authorised. If it has not been previously agreed, or exceeds the agreed limit, it is unauthorised.

Unauthorised overdrafts are very expensive, usually incurring both a high rate of interest on the borrowed money, and a fee. The bank may refuse to honour cheques written on an unauthorised overdrawn account, commonly referred to as 'bouncing' cheques. In some countries, issuing cheques when there are not sufficient funds in the account is a criminal offence.

Authorised overdrafts, agreed with the bank in advance, are charged interest at a lower rate. Some banks allow small overdrafts without charging fees to avoid infuriating a customer who might be overdrawn by a relatively low amount.

Overdrafts are a convenient but expensive way of borrowing money, and borrowers should try to restrict their use to temporary periods, and avoid unauthorised overdrafts as far as possible.

2.1.2 Credit Card Borrowing

Customers in the UK and US are very attached to their credit cards from banks and financial institutions, and other cards from retail stores, known as store cards. In other countries, including much of Europe, the use is much less widespread.

A wide variety of retail goods such as food, electrical goods, petrol and cinema tickets can be paid for using a credit card. The retailer is paid by the credit card company for the goods sold; the credit card company charges the retailer a small fee, but it enables the store to sell goods to customers using their credit cards.

Customers are typically sent a monthly statement by the credit card company. Customers can then choose to pay all the money owed to the credit card company, or just a percentage of the total sum owed. Interest is charged on the balance owed by the customer.

Generally, the interest rate charged on credit cards is relatively high compared to other forms of borrowing, including overdrafts. However, if a credit card customer pays the full balance each month, he is borrowing interest-free. It is also common for credit card companies to offer 0% interest to new customers for balances transferred from other cards and for new purchases for a set period, often six months.

2.1.3 Loans

Loans can be subdivided into two groups: secured or unsecured.

Unsecured loans are typically used to purchase items such as a new kitchen. The lender will check the creditworthiness of the borrower – assessing whether he can afford to repay the loan and interest over the agreed term of, say, 48 months from his income, given his existing outgoings.

The unsecured loan is not linked to the item that is purchased with the loan (in contrast to mortgages which are covered in Section 3), so if the borrower defaults it can be difficult for the lender to enforce repayment. The usual mechanism for the unsecured lender to enforce repayment is to start legal proceedings to get the money back.

Example

Jerry borrows £10,000, unsecured over a 36-month period, to buy a new kitchen. After three months, Jerry loses his job and is unable to continue to meet the repayments and interest. Because the loan is unsecured, the lender is not able to take the kitchen to recoup the money. The lender can simply negotiate with Jerry to reschedule the repayments, or commence legal proceedings to reclaim the money owed.

It is common for loans made to buy property to be secured. Such loans are referred to as **mortgages**, and the security provided to the lender means that the rate of interest is likely to be lower than on other forms of borrowing, such as overdrafts and unsecured loans. If secured loans are not repaid, the lender can repossess the specific property which was the security for the loan.

Example

Jenny borrows £500,000 to buy a house. The loan is secured on the property. Jenny loses her job and is unable to continue to meet the repayments and interest. Because the loan is secured, the lender is able to take the house to recoup the money. If the lender takes this route, the house will be sold and the lender will take the amount owed and give the rest, if any, to Jenny.

For more detail on mortgages, see Section 3.

2.2 Interest Rates

Learning Objective

9.2.2 Know the difference between the quoted interest rate on borrowing and the effective annual percentage rate of borrowing

9.2.3 Be able to calculate the effective annual percentage rate of borrowing, given the quoted interest rate and frequency of payment

---

As seen in the previous section, the costs of borrowing vary depending on the form of borrowing, how long the money is required for, the security offered and the amount borrowed.

Mortgages, secured on a house, are much cheaper than credit cards and agreed overdrafts.

Unauthorised overdrafts are incredibly expensive and can be thought of as a fine that the bank charges for not keeping it fully informed of spending excesses.

Borrowers also have to grapple with the different rates quoted by lenders – loan companies traditionally quote flat rates that are lower than the true rate or **effective annual rate (EAR)**.

Example

The Moneybags Credit Card Company might quote their interest rate at 12% per annum, charged on a quarterly basis.

The EAR can be determined by taking the quoted rate and dividing by four (to represent the quarterly charge). It is this rate that is applied to the amount borrowed on a quarterly basis; 12% divided by 4 = 3%.

Imagine an individual borrows US$100 on his Moneybags credit card. Assuming he makes no repayments for a year, how much will be owed?

At the end of the first quarter US$100 x 3% = US$3 will be added to the balance outstanding, to make it US$103.

At the end of the second quarter, interest will be due on both the original borrowing and the interest. In other words there will be interest charged on the first quarter's interest of US$3, as well as the US$100 original borrowing: US$103 x 3% = US$3.09 will be added to make the outstanding balance US$106.09.

At the end of the third quarter, interest will be charged at 3% on the amount outstanding (including the first and second quarters' interest). US$106.09 x 3% = US$3.18 will be added to make the outstanding balance US$109.27.

At the end of the fourth quarter, interest will be charged at 3% on the amount outstanding (including the first, second and third quarters' interest). US$109.27 x 3% = US$3.28 will be added to make the outstanding balance US$112.55.

In total the interest incurred on the US$100 was US$12.55 over the year. This is an EAR of 12.55 ÷ 100 x 100 = 12.55%.

There is a shortcut method to arrive at the effective annual rate seen above. It is simply to take the quoted rate, divide by the appropriate frequency (four for quarterly, two for half-yearly, 12 for monthly), and express the result as a decimal – in other words, 3% will be expressed as 0.03, 6% as 0.06, etc.

The decimal is then added to 1 and multiplied by itself by the appropriate frequency. The result minus 1, and multiplied by 100, is the EAR.

From the example above:

- 12% divided by 4 = 3%, expressed as 0.03.
- 1 + 0.03 = 1.03.
- 1.03^4 = 1.03 x 1.03 x 1.03 x 1.03 = 1.1255.
- 1.1255 – 1 = 0.1255 x 100 = 12.55%.

This formula can also be applied to deposits to determine the EAR of a deposit paying interest at regular intervals.

To make comparisons easier, lenders must quote the true cost of borrowing, embracing the EAR and including any fees that are required to be paid by the borrower. This is known as the **annual percentage rate (APR)**. The additional fees that the lender adds to the cost of borrowing might be, for example, loan arrangement fees.

3. Mortgages

Learning Objective

9.3.1 Understand the characteristics of the mortgage market: interest rates; repayment

---

3.1 Characteristics of the Property Market and Mortgages

A mortgage is simply a secured loan, with the security taking the form of a property.

A mortgage is typically provided to finance the purchase of a property. For most people their main form of borrowing is their mortgage on their house or flat. Mortgages tend to be over a longer term than unsecured loans, with most mortgages running for 20 or 25 years.

As well as buying your home, some of the more wealthy might take out additional mortgages to buy holiday homes. Others might take out a 'buy-to-let' mortgage loan with a view to letting the property out to tenants.

Because of the spectacular performance of property prices in many parts of the world over the last 30–40 years, property is seen as a reasonably safe investment that should provide reasonable returns as long as it is held for a considerable time. There is also potentially an additional attraction that any capital gains made on your home (often described as your 'principal private residence' by the tax authorities) are commonly not subject to any capital taxes, such as capital gains tax (CGT).

However, the costs of purchasing a property are substantial, including professional fees paid to a solicitor and a building surveyor. Each individual property is also unique, and the attractiveness or otherwise is driven heavily by personal preference. As has been seen recently, property market falls, or even crashes, are also not unknown or inconceivable, so investors should not assume that property will outperform other investments indefinitely.

Whether a mortgage is to buy a house or flat to live in, or to 'buy-to-let', the factors considered by the lender are much the same. The mortgage lender, such as a bank, will consider each application for a loan in terms of the credit risk – the risk of not being repaid the principal sum loaned and the interest due.

Applicants are assessed in terms of:

- income and security of employment;
- existing outgoings – such as utility bills, other household expenses and school fees; and
- the size of the loan in relation to the value of the property being purchased. This is referred to as the **loan-to-value** ratio.

A second mortgage is sometimes taken out on a single property. If the borrower defaults on his borrowings, the first mortgage ranks ahead of the second one in terms of being repaid out of the proceeds of the property sale.

3.2 Types of Mortgage

The most straightforward form of mortgage is a **repayment mortgage**. This is simply when the borrower will make monthly payments to the lender, with each monthly payment comprising both interest and capital.

Example

Mr Mullergee borrows £100,000 from XYZ Bank to finance the purchase of a flat on a repayment basis over 25 years. Each month he is required to pay £600 to XYZ Bank. In the above example, Mr Mullergee will pay a total of £180,000 (£600 x 12 months x 25 years) to XYZ Bank, including £80,000 interest over and above the capital borrowed of £100,000. Each payment he makes will be partly allocated to interest and partly allocated to capital. In the early years the payments are predominantly interest. Towards the middle of the term the capital begins to reduce significantly, and at the end of the mortgage term the payments are predominantly capital.

The key advantage of a repayment mortgage over other forms of mortgage is that, as long as the borrower meets the repayments each month, he is guaranteed to pay off the loan over the term of the mortgage. The main risks attached to a repayment mortgage from the borrower's perspective are:

- The cost of servicing the loan could increase, since most repayment mortgages charge interest at the lender's standard variable rate of interest. This rate of interest will increase if interest rates go up.
- The borrower runs the risk of having the property repossessed if he fails to meet the repayments – remember, the mortgage loan is secured on the underlying property.

3.3 Payment Terms

There are four main methods by which the interest on a mortgage may be charged:

- variable rate;
- fixed rate;
- capped rate; and
- discounted rate.

Variable Rate Mortgages	• In a standard variable rate mortgage the borrower pays interest at a rate that varies with prevailing interest rates. The lender's standard variable rates will reflect increases or decreases in base rates. • Once they have entered into a variable rate mortgage, the borrower will benefit from rates falling and remaining low, but will suffer the additional costs when rates increase. The interest rate charged may also track the movement in the official base rate, when it is known as a 'tracker' mortgage.
Fixed Rate Mortgages	• In a fixed rate mortgage the borrower's interest rate is set for an initial period, such as the first three or five years. • If interest rates rise, the borrower is protected from the higher rates throughout this period, continuing to pay the lower, fixed, rate of interest. However, if rates fall and perhaps stay low, the fixed rate loan can only be cancelled if a redemption penalty is paid. The penalty is calculated to recoup the loss suffered by the lender as a result of the cancellation of the fixed rate loan. • It is common for fixed rate borrowers to be required to remain with the lender and pay interest at the lender's standard variable rate for a few years after the fixed rate deal ends – commonly referred to as a 'lock in' period.
Capped Rate Mortgages	• Capped mortgages protect borrowers from rates rising above a particular rate – the 'capped rate'. • For example, a mortgage might be taken out at 6%, with the interest rate based on the lender's standard variable rate, but with a cap at 7%. If prevailing rates fall to 5%, the borrower pays at that rate; but if rates rise to 8% the rate paid cannot rise above the cap, and is only 7%.
Discounted Rate Mortgages	• Lending institutions often attract borrowers by offering discounted rate mortgages. A 6% loan might be discounted to 5% for the first three years. • Such deals might attract 'switchers' – borrowers who shop around and remortgage at a better rate. They may also be useful for first-time buyers as they make the transition to home ownership with a relatively low but growing level of income.

3.4 Islamic Finance

Learning Objective

9.3.2 Know the prohibition on interest under Islamic finance and the types of mortgage contracts

Islamic law, the Sharia'a, bans the payment or receipt of interest and, as a result, rules out the use of traditional western loans and mortgages for buying property.

Financial institutions have, however, been keen to develop mortgage schemes that avoid interest payments and can therefore be used by Muslims.

Sharia'a-compliant mortgages come in two forms: the ijara and the murabaha. Both are carefully structured deals that avoid the use of interest payments, but still allow the financial institution to make a profit.

Under the **ijara** system, the bank rather than the borrower buys the property. The customer rents the home from the bank for 25 years and the payments made during that time add up to the original price plus the bank's profit. Rent reviews are undertaken periodically, say six-monthly. Once the final payment is made, ownership of the property is transferred to the customer. Since no interest is being paid, the arrangement complies with Islamic law.

With the **murabaha** system, the bank also buys the property but then sells it on to the customer at a higher price. The buyer repays the higher figure in a series of instalments, typically over a 15-year period. Since only the capital is being repaid, there is no interest.

Islamic finance extends, of course, well beyond just mortgages and is one of the fastest-growing financial areas.

4. Life Assurance

Life assurance and protection policies are designed and sold by the insurance industry to provide individuals with some financial protection in case certain events occur. Although product details may vary from country to country, the general principles of what the individual (and his adviser) should be looking for in the products and their main features tend to be consistent.

4.1 Life Cover

Learning Objective

9.4.1 Understand the basic principles of life assurance

A life policy is simply an insurance policy where the event insured is a death. Such policies involve the payment of premiums in exchange for life cover – a lump sum that is payable upon death.

Instead of paying a fixed sum on death, there are investment-based policies which may pay a sum calculated as a guaranteed amount plus any profits made during the period between the policy being taken out and the death of the insured. The total paid out, therefore, depends on the guaranteed sum, the date of death and the investment performance of the fund.

Before looking at the types of policies available, it is important to understand some key terms.

Key Terms	
Proposer	The person who proposes to enter into a contract of insurance with a life insurance company to insure himself or another person on whose life he has insurable interest.
Life Assured	The person on whose life the contract depends is called the 'life assured'. Although the person who owns the policy and the life assured are frequently the same person, this is not necessarily the case. A policy on the life of one person, but effected and owned by someone else, is called a 'life of another' policy. A policy effected by the life assured is called an 'own life policy'.
Single Life	A single life policy pays out on one individual's death.
Joint Life	When cover is required for two people, this can typically be arranged in one of two ways: through a joint life policy or two single life policies.
	A joint life policy can be arranged so that the benefits would be paid out following the death of either the first, or, if required for a specific reason, the second life assured. The majority of policies are arranged ultimately to protect financial dependants, with the sum assured or benefits being paid on the first death.
	With two separate single life policies, each person is covered separately. If both lives assured were to die at the same time, as the result of a car accident for example, the full benefits would be payable on each of the policies. If one of the lives assured died, benefits would be paid for that policy, with the surviving partner having continuing cover on their life.
Insurable Interest	To buy a life insurance policy on someone else's life, the proposer must have an interest in that person remaining alive, or expect financial loss from that person's death. This is called an 'insurable interest'.

There are two types of life cover we need to consider, namely whole-of-life assurance and term assurance. A **whole-of-life policy** provides permanent cover, meaning that the sum assured will be paid whenever death occurs, as opposed to if death occurs within the term of a **term assurance policy**.

4.2 Whole-of-Life Assurance

Learning Objective

9.4.2 Know the main types of life policy: term assurance; whole-of-life

There are three types of whole-of-life policy:

- **non-profit** that is for a guaranteed sum only;
- **with-profits**, which pays a guaranteed amount plus any profits made during the period between the policy being taken out and death;
- **unit-linked policies** where the return will be directly related to the investment performance of the units in the insurance company's fund.

In **a non-profit policy** the insured sum is chosen at the outset and is fixed. For example, £500,000 payable on death.

With-profits funds are used to build up a sum of money for retirement, to pay off the capital of a mortgage, or to insure against an event such as death. One advantage of with-profits schemes is that profits are locked in each year. If an investor bought shares or bonds directly, or within a mutual fund, the value of the investments could fall just as they are needed because of general declines in the stock market. With-profits schemes avoid this risk by smoothing the returns. A typical scheme might pay out:

- the **sum assured** or **guaranteed sum**, which is usually an amount a little less than the premiums paid over the term;
- **annual bonuses**, which are declared each year by the insurance company, and which can vary. If the underlying performance of the investments in the fund is better than expected, this is a good year, and a part of the surplus will be held back to enable the insurance company to award an annual bonus in a bad year. In this way, the returns smooth out the peaks and troughs that may be occurring in the underlying stock market;
- a **terminal bonus** at the end of the period. This could be substantial, for example 20% of the sum insured, but is not declared until the end of the policy term.

The final kind of policy is a **unit-linked** or **unitised** scheme. Each month, premiums are used to purchase units in an investment fund. Some units are then used to purchase term insurance and the rest remain invested in the investment fund run by the insurance company. When it is held to fund a mortgage, the insurance company will review the policies every five or ten years, making the investor aware of any potential shortfall and perhaps suggesting an increase in the premiums to boost the life cover or the guaranteed sum.

The reason for such policies being taken out is not normally just for the insured sum itself. Usually they are bought as part of a protection planning exercise, to provide a lump sum in the event of death to pay off the principal in a mortgage or to provide funds to assist with the payment of any tax that might become payable on death. They can serve two purposes, therefore: both protection and investment.

Purchasing a life assurance policy is the same as entering into any other contract. When a person completes a proposal form and submits it to an insurance company, that constitutes a part of the formal process of entering into a contract. The principle of utmost good faith applies to insurance contracts. This places an obligation on the person seeking insurance to disclose any material facts that may affect how the insurance company may judge the risk of the contract they are entering into. Failure to disclose a material fact gives the insurance company the right to avoid paying out in the event of a claim.

There are a wide range of variations on the basic life policy that are driven by mortality risk, investment and expenses and premium options – all of which impact on the structure of the policy itself.

4.3 Term Assurance

Learning Objective

9.4.2 Know the main types of life policy: term assurance; whole-of-life

Term assurance is a type of policy that pays out a lump sum in the event of death occurring within a specified period. (Technically, the term 'life assurance' should be used to refer to a whole-of-life policy that will pay out on death, while life insurance should be used in the context of term policies that pay out only if death occurs within a particular period.)

Term assurance has a variety of uses, such as ensuring there are funds available to repay a mortgage in case someone dies or providing a lump sum that can be used to generate income for a surviving partner or to provide funds to pay any tax that might become payable on death.

When taking out life cover, the individual selects the amount that they wish to be paid out if the event happens, and the period that they want the cover to run for. If, during the period when the cover is in place, they die, then a lump sum will be paid out that equals the amount of life cover selected. With some policies, if an individual is diagnosed as suffering from a terminal illness which is expected to cause death within 12 months of the diagnosis, then the lump sum is payable at that point.

The amount of the premiums paid for term assurance will depend on:

- the amount insured;
- age, sex and family history;
- other risk factors, including state of health (for example, whether the individual is a smoker or non-smoker), his occupation and whether he participates in dangerous sports such as hang-gliding; and
- the term over which cover is required.

When selecting the amount of cover, an individual is able to choose three types of cover, namely level, increasing or decreasing cover.

Level Cover	• Level cover, as the name suggests, means that the amount to be paid out if the event happens remains the same throughout the period in which the policy is in force. As a result, the premiums are fixed at the outset and do not change during the period of the policy.
Increasing Cover	• With increasing cover, the amount of cover and the premium increase on each anniversary of the taking out of the policy. The amount by which the cover will increase will be determined at the outset and can be an amount that is the same as the change in the consumer prices index, so that the cover maintains its real value after allowing for inflation. The premium paid will also increase, and the rate of increase will be determined at the start of the policy.
Decreasing Cover	• As you would expect, with decreasing cover the amount that is originally chosen as the sum to be paid out decreases each year. The amount by which it decreases is agreed at the outset and, if it is used to repay a mortgage, it will be based on the expected reduction in the outstanding mortgage that would occur if the client had a repayment mortgage. Although the amount of cover will diminish year-by-year, the premiums payable will remain the same throughout the policy.

End of Chapter Questions

Think of an answer for each question and refer to the appropriate section for confirmation.

1. What is the difference between a defined benefit pension scheme and a defined contribution pension scheme?
   Answer Reference: Section 1.3

2. When can a lender repossess the specific property which was purchased with a loan?
   Answer Reference: Section 2.1.3

3. How can the interest rates on different types of loans or accounts be readily compared?
   Answer Reference: Section 2.2

4. Firm A charges interest annually at 6% pa on loans and Firm B charges interest quarterly at 6% pa. Which is the more expensive?
   Answer Reference: Section 2.2

5. Your firm offers fixed rate loans at 6% pa charged quarterly. Ignoring charges, what is the APR on the loan?
   Answer Reference: Section 2.2

6. What are the principal risks associated with interest-only mortgages?
   Answer Reference: Section 3.2

7. What are the main differences between the different ways in which interest is calculated on mortgages?
   Answer Reference: Section 3.3

8. What are the key differences between non-profit, with-profits and unit-linked policies?
   Answer Reference: Section 4.2

9. What are the main factors that will influence the premium for a term assurance policy?
   Answer Reference: Section 4.3

10. What are the main differences between life assurance and term assurance?
    Answer Reference: Sections 4.1–4.3

Glossary and Abbreviations

Active Management

A type of investment approach employed to generate returns in excess of the market.

Annual General Meeting (AGM)

Yearly meeting of shareholders. Mainly used to vote on dividends, appoint directors and approve financial statements. Also referred to as a stockholder meeting or an Annual General Assembly in some jurisdictions.

Articles of Association

The legal document which sets out the internal constitution of a company. Included within the articles will be details of shareholder voting rights and company borrowing powers.

Auction

System used to issue securities when the successful applicants pay the price that they bid. Examples of its use include the UK Debt Management Office (DMO) when it issues gilts.

Authorisation

Required status in the UK for firms that want to provide financial services.

Authorised Corporate Director (ACD)

Fund manager for an open-ended investment company (OEIC).

Balance of Payments

A summary of all the transactions between a country and the rest of the world. The difference between a country's imports and exports.

Bank of England

The UK's central bank. Implements economic policy decided by the Treasury and determines interest rates.

Bearer Securities

Those whose ownership is evidenced by the mere possession of a certificate. Ownership can, therefore, pass from hand to hand without any formalities.

Bid Price

Bond and share prices are quoted as bid and offer. The bid is the lower of the two prices and is the one that would be received when selling.

Bonds

Debt securities which typically entitle holders to annual interest and repayment at maturity. Commonly issued by both companies and governments.

Bonus Issue

A free issue of shares to existing shareholders. No money is paid. The share price falls pro rata. Also known as a capitalisation or scrip issue.

Broker/Dealer

Member firm of a stock exchange.

CAC 40

Index of the prices of major French company shares.

Call Option

Option giving its buyer the right to buy an asset at an agreed price.

Capital Gains Tax (CGT)

Tax payable by individuals on profit made on the disposal of certain assets.

Capitalisation Issue

See Bonus Issue.

Central Bank

Central banks typically have responsibility for setting a country's or a region's short-term interest rate, controlling the money supply, acting as banker and lender of last resort to the banking system and managing the national debt.

Certificated

Ownership (of shares) designated by certificate.

Certificates of Deposit (CDs)

Certificates issued by a bank as evidence that interest-bearing funds have been deposited with it. CDs are traded within the money market.

Clean Price

The quoted price of a bond. The clean price excludes accrued interest or interest to be deducted, as appropriate.

Closed-Ended

Organisations such as companies which are a fixed size as determined by their share capital. Commonly used to distinguish investment trusts (closed-ended) from unit trusts and OEICs (open-ended).

Closing

Reversing an original position by, for example, selling what you have previously bought.

Commercial Paper (CP)

Money market instrument issued by large corporates.

Commission

Charges for acting as agent or broker.

Commodity

Items including sugar, wheat, oil and copper. Derivatives of commodities are traded on exchanges (eg, oil futures on Intercontinental Exchange [ICE] Futures).

Consumer Prices Index (CPI)

Index that measures the movement of prices faced by a typical consumer.

Contract

A standard unit of trading in derivatives.

Convertible Bond

A bond which can be convertible, at the investor's choice, into the same company's shares.

Coupon

Amount of interest paid on a bond.

Credit Creation

Expansion of loans which increases the money supply.

CREST

Electronic settlement system used to settle transactions for UK and Irish shares plus some other international shares.

Data Protection

Legislation regulating the use of client data.

Debt Management Office (DMO)

UK agency responsible for issuing gilts on behalf of the Treasury.

Dematerialised (Form)

System where securities are held electronically without certificates.

Derivatives

Options, futures and swaps. Their price is derived from an underlying asset.

Dirty Price

The price of a bond inclusive of accrued interest or exclusive of interest to be deducted, as appropriate.

Diversification

Investment strategy of spreading risk by investing in a range of investments.

Dividend

Distribution of profits by a company.

Dividend Yield

Most recent dividend as a percentage of current share price.

Dow Jones Index

Major share index in the USA, based on the prices of 30 major company shares.

Dual Pricing

System in which a unit trust manager quotes two prices at which investors can sell and buy.

Economic Cycle

The course an economy conventionally takes as economic growth fluctuates over time. Also known as the business cycle.

Economic Growth

The growth of GDP (gross domestic product) or GNP (gross national product) expressed in real terms, usually over the course of a calendar year. Often used as a barometer of an economy's health.

Effective Rate

The annualised compound rate of interest applied to a cash deposit. Also known as the Annual Equivalent Rate (AER).

Equity

Another name for shares. Shares represent the equity interest (assets minus liabilities) of the shareholders of the company.

Eurobond

An interest-bearing security issued internationally.

Euronext

European stock exchange network formed by the merger of the Paris, Brussels, Amsterdam and Lisbon exchanges and which has merged with the New York Stock Exchange (NYSE). Now part of the ICE (Intercontinental Exchange) group.

Exchange

Marketplace for trading investments.

Exchange Rate

The rate at which one currency can be exchanged for another.

Ex-Dividend (xd)

The period during which the purchase of shares or bonds (on which a dividend or coupon payment has been declared) does not entitle the new holder to this next dividend or interest payment.

Exercise an Option

Take up the right to buy or sell the underlying asset in an option.

Exercise Price

The price at which the right conferred by an option can be exercised by the holder against the writer.

Financial Conduct Authority (FCA)

One of the UK bodies that replaced the FSA in 2013 and is responsible for regulation of conduct in retail and wholesale, financial markets and the infrastructure that supports those markets.

Fiscal Policy

The use of government spending, taxation and borrowing policies to either boost or restrain domestic demand in the economy so as to maintain full employment and price stability.

Fiscal Years

These are the periods of assessment for income tax and CGT. In some countries, fiscal years are the same as calendar years. In others alternative dates are used, eg, UK fiscal years run from 6 April to 5 April.

Fixed Interest Security

A tradeable negotiable instrument, issued by a borrower for a fixed term, during which a regular and predetermined fixed rate of interest based upon a nominal value is paid to the holder until it is redeemed and the principal is repaid.

Fixed Rate Borrowing

Borrowing when a set interest rate is paid.

Floating Rate Notes (FRNs)

Debt securities issued with a coupon periodically referenced to a benchmark interest rate.

Forex

Abbreviation for foreign exchange trading.

Forward

A derivatives contract that creates a legally binding obligation between two parties for one to buy and the other to sell a pre-specified amount of an asset at a pre-specified price on a pre-specified future date. As individually negotiated contracts, forwards are not traded on a derivatives exchange.

Forward Exchange Rate

An exchange rate set today, embodied in a forward contract, that will apply to a foreign exchange transaction at some pre-specified point in the future.

FTSE 100

Main UK share index of 100 leading shares ('Footsie').

FTSE All Share Index

Index comprising around 98% of UK listed shares by value.

Fund Manager

Firm that invests money on behalf of customers.

Future

An agreement to buy or sell an item at a future date, at a price agreed today. Differs from a forward in that it is a standardised amount and therefore the contract can be traded on an exchange.

Gilt-Edged Security

UK government bond.

Gross Domestic Product (GDP)

A measure of a country's output.

Gross National Product (GNP)

Gross domestic product adjusted for income earned by residents from overseas investments and income earned in the UK by foreign investors.

Gross Redemption Yield (GRY)

The annual compound return from holding a bond to maturity, taking into account both interest payments and any capital gain or loss at maturity.

Harmonised Index of Consumer Prices (HICP)

Standard measurement of inflation throughout the EU.

Hedging

A technique employed to reduce the impact of adverse price movements on financial assets held.

Holder

Investor who buys put or call options.

Inflation

An increase in the general level of prices.

Inheritance Tax (IHT)

UK estate tax on the value of an estate when a person dies.

Initial Public Offering (IPO)

A new issue of ordinary shares whether made by an offer for sale, an offer for subscription or a placing. Also known as a new issue.

Insider Dealing/Trading

Criminal offence by people with unpublished price-sensitive information who deal, advise others to deal or pass the information on.

Integration

Third stage of money laundering.

Intercontinental Exchange (ICE)

Intercontinental Exchange operates regulated global futures exchanges and over-the-counter (OTC) markets for agricultural, energy, equity index and currency contracts, as well as credit derivatives. ICE conducts its energy futures markets through ICE Futures Europe, which is based in London.

Investment Bank

Business that specialises in raising debt and equity for companies.

Investment Company with Variable Capital (ICVC)

Alternative term for an OEIC.

Investment Trust

A company, not a trust, which invests in a diversified range of investments.

Layering

Second stage in money laundering.

LIFFE

The UK's principal derivatives exchange for trading financial and soft commodity derivatives products. Now owned by ICE.

LIFFE CONNECT™

Order-driven trading system on LIFFE.

Limit Order

An order placed on a market which specifies the highest price it will pay (for a buy order) or the lowest price it will accept (for a sell order).

Liquidity

Ease with which an item can be traded on the market. Liquid markets are described as deep.

Liquidity Risk

The risk that shares may be difficult to sell at a reasonable price.

Listing

Companies whose securities are listed on the London Stock Exchange (LSE) and available to be traded.

Lloyd's of London

The world's largest insurance market.

Loan Stock

A corporate bond issued in the domestic bond market without any underlying collateral, or security.

London Interbank Offered Rate (LIBOR)

A benchmark money market interest rate.

London Metal Exchange (LME)

The market for trading in derivatives of certain metals; such as copper, zinc and aluminium.

London Stock Exchange (LSE)

The main UK market for securities.

Long Position

The position following the purchase of a security or buying a derivative.

Market

All exchanges are markets – electronic or physical meeting places where assets are bought or sold.

Market Capitalisation

Total market value of a company's shares.

Market Maker

A stock exchange member firm which quotes prices and trades stocks during the mandatory quote period.

Maturity

Date when the capital on a bond is repaid.

Memorandum of Association

The legal document that principally defines a company's powers, or objects, and its relationship with the outside world. The Memorandum also details the number and nominal value of shares the company is authorised to issue and has issued.

Mixed Economy

Economy which works through a combination of market forces and government involvement.

Monetary Policy

The setting of short-term interest rates by a central bank in order to manage domestic demand and achieve price stability in the economy.

Monetary Policy Committee (MPC)

Committee run by the Bank of England which sets UK interest rates.

Multilateral Trading Facilities (MTFs)

Systems that bring together multiple parties that are interested in buying and selling financial instruments including shares, bonds and derivatives.

Names

Participants at Lloyd's of London who form syndicates to write insurance business. Both individuals and companies can be names.

NASDAQ

US market specialising in the shares of technology companies.

NASDAQ Composite

NASDAQ stock index.

National Debt

A government's total outstanding borrowing resulting from financing successive budget deficits, mainly through the issue of government-backed securities.

Nikkei 225

The main Japanese share index.

Nominal Value

The amount of a bond that will be repaid on maturity. Also known as face or par value.

Offer Price

Bond and share prices are quoted as bid and offer. The offer is the higher of the two prices and is the one that would be received when buying.

Open

Initiate a transaction, eg, an opening purchase or sale of a future. Normally reversed by a closing transaction.

Open Economy

Country with no restrictions on trading with other countries.

Open-Ended

Type of investment, such as OEICs or unit trusts, which can expand without limit.

Open-Ended Investment Company (OEIC)

Collective investment vehicle similar to unit trusts. Alternatively described as an ICVC (investment company with variable capital).

Open Outcry

Trading system used by some derivatives exchanges. Participants stand on the floor of the exchange and call out transactions they would like to undertake.

Opening

Undertaking a transaction which creates a long or short position.

Option

A derivative giving the buyer the right, but not the obligation, to buy or sell an asset.

Over-the-Counter (OTC) Derivatives

Derivatives that are not traded on a derivatives exchange owing to their non-standardised contract specifications.

Passive Management

An investment approach employed in those securities markets that are believed to be price-efficient.

Placement

First stage of money laundering.

Pre-Emption Rights

The rights accorded to ordinary shareholders under company law to subscribe for new ordinary shares issued by the company, in which they have the shareholding, for cash before the shares are offered to outside investors.

Preference Share

Shares which pay fixed dividends. Shareholders do not have voting rights, but do have preference over ordinary shares in default situations.

Premium

The amount of cash paid by the holder of an option to the writer in exchange for conferring a right.

Primary Market

The function of a stock exchange in bringing securities to the market and raising funds.

Proxy

Appointee who votes on a shareholder's behalf at company meetings.

Prudential Regulation Authority (PRA)

The UK body responsible for prudential regulation of all deposit-taking institutions, insurers and investment banks.

Put Option

Option when buyer has the right to sell an asset.

Quote-Driven

Dealing system driven by securities firms who quote buying and selling prices.

Real Estate Investment Trust (REIT)

An investment trust that specialises in investing in commercial property.

Redeemable Security

A security issued with a known maturity, or redemption, date.

Redemption

The repayment of principal to the holder of a redeemable security.

Registrar

An official of a company who maintains the share register.

Repo

The sale and repurchase of bonds between two parties, with the repurchase being made at a price and date fixed in advance.

Resolution

Proposal on which shareholders vote.

Retail Bank

Organisation that provides banking facilities to individuals and small/medium businesses.

Retail Prices Index (RPI)

Index that measures the movement of prices faced by retail consumers in the UK.

Rights Issue

The issue of new ordinary shares to a company's shareholders in proportion to each shareholder's existing shareholding, usually at a price deeply discounted to that prevailing in the market.

RPIX

UK index that shows the underlying rate of inflation, excluding the impact of mortgage payments.

Scrip Issue

See Bonus Issue.

Secondary Market

Marketplace for trading in existing securities.

Securities

Bonds and equities.

Shares

Shares are the equity capital of a company, hence the reason they are referred to as equities. They may comprise ordinary shares and preference shares or may be referred to as common shares or preferred stock.

Share Capital

The nominal value of a company's equity or ordinary shares. A company's authorised share capital is the nominal value of equity the company may issue, while issued share capital is that which the company has issued. The term share capital is often extended to include a company's preference shares.

Short Position

The position following the sale of a security not owned or selling a derivative.

Single Pricing

Refers to the use of the mid-market price of the underlying assets to produce a single price for units/shares in collective investment schemes.

Special Resolution

Proposal put to shareholders requiring 75% of the votes cast.

Spread

Difference between a buying (bid) and selling (ask or offer) price.

State-Controlled Economy

Country where all economic activity is controlled by the state.

Stocks

See Shares.

Stock Exchange Electronic Trading System (SETS)

The LSE's electronic order-driven trading system for the UK's main companies.

Swap

An OTC derivative whereby two parties exchange a series of periodic payments based on a notional principal amount over an agreed term. Swaps can take the form of interest rate swaps, currency swaps and equity swaps.

Takeover

When one company buys more than 50% of the shares of another.

Third Party Administrator

A firm that specialises in undertaking investment administration for other firms.

Treasury

Government department ultimately responsible for the regulation of the financial services industry.

Treasury Bills

Short-term (usually 90-day) borrowings of the government. Issued at a discount to the nominal value at which they will mature. Traded in the money market.

Two-Way Price

Prices quoted by a market maker at which they are willing to buy (bid) and sell (offer).

Underlying

Asset from which a derivative is derived.

Unit Trust

A system whereby money from investors is pooled together and invested collectively on their behalf into an open-ended trust.

Writer

Party selling an option. The writers receive premiums in exchange for taking the risk of being exercised against.

Xetra Dax

German shares index, comprising 30 shares.

Yield

Income from an investment as a percentage of the current price.

Yield Curve

The depiction of the relationship between the yields and the maturity of bonds of the same type.

Zero Coupon Bonds (ZCBs)

Bonds issued at a discount to their nominal value that do not pay a coupon but which are redeemed at par on a pre-specified future date.

ABS	Asset-Backed Security
ACD	Authorised Corporate Director
ADR	American Depositary Receipt
AER	Annual Effective Rate
AGM	Annual General Meeting
APR	Annual Percentage Rate
BIS	Bank for International Settlements
BoJ	Bank of Japan
CBOE	Chicago Board Options Exchange
CBOT	Chicago Board of Trade
CD	Certificate of Deposit
CCP	Central Counterparty
CDS	Credit Default Swap
CGT	Capital Gains Tax
CME	Chicago Mercantile Exchange
CP	Commercial Paper
CPI	Consumer Price Index
CSRC	Chinese Securities Regulatory Commission
DFSA	Dubai Financial Services Authority
DJIA	Dow Jones Industrial Average
DMO	Debt Management Office
DTTC	Depository Trust & Clearing Corporation
DVP	Delivery Versus Payment
EAR	Effective Annual Rate
ECB	European Central Bank
EMU	Economic and Monetary Union
ESMA	European Securities and Markets Authority
ETF	Exchange-Traded Fund
EU	European Union
FCA	Financial Conduct Authority
FATF	Financial Action Task Force
FCP	Fonds Commun de Placement
FOMC	Federal Open Market Committee
FRN	Floating Rate Note
FSA	Financial Services Authority
FTSE	Financial Times Stock Exchange
GDP	Gross Domestic Product
GDR	Global Depositary Receipt
GNP	Gross National Product
GRY	Gross Redemption Yield
HICP	Harmonised Index of Consumer Prices
IBE	Institute of Business Ethics
ICE	Intercontinental Exchange
ICMA	International Capital Market Association
ICVC	Investment Companies with Variable Capital
IHT	Inheritance Tax
IOSCO	International Organization of Securities Commissions
IPO	Initial Public Offering

IRA	Individual Retirement Account
ISDA	International Swaps and Derivatives Association
ITC	Investment Trust Company
IWG	International Working Group of Sovereign Wealth Funds
JGB	Japanese Government Bond
LIBOR	London Interbank Offered Rate
LIFFE	London International Financial Futures and Options Exchange
LME	London Metal Exchange
LSE	London Stock Exchange
MLRO	Money Laundering Reporting Officer
MPC	Monetary Policy Committee
MTF	Multilateral Trading Facility
MTN	Medium-Term Note
NASDAQ	National Association of Securities Dealers Automated Quotations
NAV	Net Asset Value
NYMEX	New York Mercantile Exchange
NYSE	New York Stock Exchange
OECD	Organisation for Economic Co-operation and Development
OEIC	Open-Ended Investment Company
OPEC	Organisation of Petroleum Exporting Countries
OTC	Over-the-Counter
PLC	Public Limited Company
PRA	Prudential Regulation Authority
REIT	Real Estate Investment Trust
RPI	Retail Prices Index
RPIX	Retail Prices Index (excluding interest)
S&P	Standard & Poor's
SEAQ	Stock Exchange Automated Quotation system
SETS	Stock Exchange Electronic Trading System
SICAV	Société d'Investissement à Capital Variable
SIPP	Self-Invested Personal Pension
SPV	Special Purpose Vehicle
STRIPS	Separate Trading of Registered Interest and Principal Securities
TIPS	Treasury Inflation-Protected Securities
TPA	Third Party Administrator
TSE	Tokyo Stock Exchange
UCITS	Undertakings for Collective Investments in Transferable Securities
UIT	Unit Investment Trust
VAT	Value Added Tax
VCC	Variable Capital Company
WFE	World Federation of Exchanges
WTO	World Trade Organisation
ZCB	Zero Coupon Bond

Multiple Choice Questions

The following questions have been compiled to reflect as closely as possible the standard that you will experience in your examination. Please note, however, they are not actual exam questions.

Tick one answer for each question. When you have completed all questions, refer to the end of this section for the answers.

1. Which of the following is not a fiscal policy tool that a government would use to manage the economy?

   A. Altering tax rates
   B. Changing welfare provision
   C. Adjusting government spending
   D. Changing the interest rate

2. Holding assets in safekeeping is one of the principal activities of which of the following?

   A. Custodian bank
   B. International bank
   C. Investment bank
   D. Retail bank

3. What is the potential impact of increasing levels of government spending?

   A. A decrease in the amount of government bonds issued
   B. Falling levels of inflation
   C. Reduction in the amount of outstanding government debt
   D. Rising levels of inflation

4. Which of the following statements concerning call and put options is true?

   A. The buyer of a call has the right to sell an asset
   B. The buyer of a put has the right to buy or sell an asset
   C. The seller of a call has the right to sell an asset
   D. The buyer of a call has the right to buy an asset

5. In which type of FX transaction would you agree the exchange rate to be used today with the counterparty for a particular date, but not exchange currencies until a later time agreed between the parties?

   A. Forward
   B. Future
   C. Spot
   D. Swap

6. Which of the following is normally traded in the money markets?

   A. Treasury bill
   B. Treasury gilt
   C. Treasury note
   D. Treasury stock

7. If there is expected to be a period of declining interest rates, which mortgage payment terms are likely to be least favourable?

   A. Capped rate
   B. Discounted rate
   C. Fixed rate
   D. Variable rate

8. In the event of a company going into liquidation, who would normally have the lowest priority for payment?

   A. Banks
   B. Bond holders
   C. Ordinary shareholders
   D. Preference shareholders

9. Which of the following is not a function normally undertaken by a central bank?

   A. Controlling the money supply
   B. Lending to commercial banks
   C. Managing the national debt
   D. Regulating stock markets

10. Which of the following can be said of corporate bonds?

   A. They have market risk and default risk
   B. They have market risk but no default risk
   C. They have default risk but no market risk
   D. They have neither market risk nor default risk

11. Which of the following is hoping for the price of an asset to fall?

   A. The holder of a call option
   B. An investor who is long a future
   C. The writer of a put option
   D. An investor who is short a future

12. Which of the following types of US government security is a zero coupon instrument?

    A. Treasury note
    B. Treasury bond
    C. TIPS
    D. Treasury bill

13. If a trader deliberately gives the misleading impression that demand for a particular share is greater than it really is, this type of behaviour is likely to be classed as:

    A. Front running
    B. Product churning
    C. Money laundering
    D. Market abuse

14. If a credit card company quotes its interest rate as 20% pa, charged half-yearly, what is the effective annual rate?

    A. 20%
    B. 21%
    C. 22%
    D. 23%

15. A policy that only pays out if death occurs during the term of the policy is:

    A. An endowment plan
    B. Term assurance
    C. An income replacement plan
    D. Whole-of-life assurance

16. The equity markets of which of the following countries are represented by an index called the SSE Composite?

    A. Korea
    B. Japan
    C. China
    D. India

17. What are the corporate equivalent of Treasury bills known as?

    A. Supranational bonds
    B. Commercial paper
    C. Structured products
    D. Certificates of deposit

18. How are investment trust shares usually purchased?

    A. By application to CREST
    B. Direct from the trust manager
    C. Through an ACD
    D. On the stock market

19. Which world stock market still operates using a quote-driven system?

    A. LSE
    B. Euronext
    C. NASDAQ
    D. NYSE

20. An airline establishes an agreement via an exchange-traded instrument with an oil company to pay a specific price in three months' time for a specific quantity of fuel at that time. This type of agreement is normally called:

    A. An option
    B. A future
    C. A swap
    D. A warrant

21. An investor holds £1,000 nominal value of a 7% UK government bond trading at £97.00 What is the next gross interest payment that the investor can normally expect to receive?

    A. £28.00
    B. £33.95
    C. £35.00
    D. £36.05

22. Which of the following types of financial instrument is normally covered by the insider trading rules?

    A. Options on agricultural products
    B. Futures on energy products
    C. Technology shares
    D. OEIC shares

23. TIPS is an example of which type of government bond?

    A. Conventional
    B. STRIP
    C. Index-linked
    D. Ultra-long

24. You have a holding of £10,000 5% Treasury Stock 2020 which is currently priced at 112 and on which you receive half-yearly interest of £250. What is its flat yield?

    A. 4.44%
    B. 4.46%
    C. 4.48%
    D. 4.50%

25. Which of the following is most likely to be an example of an OTC derivative?

    A. Covered warrant
    B. Future
    C. Option
    D. Swap

26. A fund that aims to mimic the performance of an index deploys which type of investment style?

    A. Contrarian
    B. Growth
    C. Passive
    D. Thematic

27. Which of the following is an example of a discount instrument?

    A. Commercial paper
    B. Commercial property
    C. Money market account
    D. Money market fund

28. Fonds Commun de Placements are a type of:

    A. Collective investment scheme
    B. Money market instrument
    C. Agricultural commodity product
    D. Life assurance policy

29. Which of the following events is the best example of a mandatory corporate action with options?

    A. Scrip issue
    B. Takeover bid
    C. Dividend payment
    D. Rights issue

30. Which of the following products is most likely to track the performance of an index?

    A. ETF
    B. Investment trust
    C. SICAV
    D. Unit trust

31. A private equity fund is likely to use which of the following types of structure?

    A. OEIC
    B. Investment trust
    C. Limited partnership
    D. Trust

32. On what day would a share price normally be expected to fall by the amount of the dividend?

    A. Record day
    B. Ex-dividend day
    C. Dividend payday
    D. Dividend declaration date

33. A company has in issue 20 million ordinary shares of 50p nominal, originally issued at a price of £2 and currently trading at £4. It has a 1:2 capitalisation issue. How much cash will the company receive as a result of this issue?

    A. Nil
    B. £10 million
    C. £20 million
    D. £40 million

34 With which trade body would you associate the trading of OTC derivatives?

    A. ICMA
    B. ISDA
    C. SWIFT
    D. TRAX

35 With what type of activity would you associate a MTF?

    A. Agreement of forward derivative trades
    B. Currency speculation
    C. Risk sharing insurance
    D. Trading equities and bonds

36. One of the key objectives of the European Central Bank is to keep inflation (as defined by the HICP) close to, but below, what threshold rate?

    A. 2%
    B. 3%
    C. 4%
    D. 5%

37. Which of the following is the legal owner of the assets of a unit trust?

    A. ACD
    B. Depository
    C. Manager
    D. Trustee

38. All of the following are true of the differences between money market and capital market instruments except:

    A. Capital market instruments are traded and settled via exchanges, and money market instruments are not
    B. Money market instruments are usually held for a shorter term than capital market instruments
    C. Money market instruments are all bearer instruments, whereas capital market instruments are more usually certificated and registered
    D. The money markets have a high minimum subscription level and are not suitable for private investors to invest in directly

39. When an annual general meeting includes a proposal to change the company's constitution, what minimum proportion of votes is normally required to carry it through?

    A. 51%
    B. 67%
    C. 75%
    D. 90%

40. The key difference between the primary market and the secondary market is that:

    A. The primary market relates to equities and the secondary market relates to bonds
    B. The primary market covers regulated and protected activities and the secondary market covers unregulated and unprotected activities
    C. The primary market is where new shares are first marketed and the secondary market is where existing shares are subsequently traded
    D. The primary market involves domestic trading and the secondary market involves overseas trading

41. A bond with a coupon of 5%, redeemable in 2020, is currently trading at US$80 per US$100 nominal. What would be the impact on the flat yield if the price increases by US$5?

    A. It would rise from 5.88% to 6.25%
    B. It would rise from 6.25% to 6.75%
    C. It would fall from 6.25% to 5.88%
    D. It would fall from 6.75% to 6.25%

42. What term is used to describe a situation where a trader has committed to buy, and is currently holding, a future which has two weeks until the specified future date?

    A. Call
    B. Put
    C. Long
    D. Short

43. A money launderer is actively switching funds between products. At what stage of money laundering would you expect to see this?

    A. Investment
    B. Integration
    C. Layering
    D. Placement

44. 70% of a fund's assets are indexed to the S&P 500 and the balance is actively managed. This type of investment approach is normally known as:

    A. Controlled growth management
    B. Momentum investment management
    C. Core satellite management
    D. Differential strategy management

45. Which of the following types of investment vehicle is most likely to be highly geared?

    A. Hedge funds
    B. Real estate investment trusts
    C. Unit trusts
    D. Open-ended investment companies

46. A retail investor has placed $10,000 on deposit at a rate of 2.5% net. What would the gross amount of interest be, assuming that 20% tax has been deducted at source?

    A. $62.50
    B. $200.00
    C. $250.00
    D. $312.50

47. What is the likely effect of inflation?

    A. Borrowers can be expected to suffer during a period of inflation
    B. Incomes which increase in line with inflation will pay less tax
    C. Lenders will receive a higher value in real terms on redemption of debts
    D. Fixed income returns will suffer during a period of inflation

48. When a client uses an 'ijara' arrangement to borrow money to acquire a property, what proportion of the property will the bank normally buy at outset?

    A. None
    B. A variable amount between 10% and 25%
    C. 50%
    D. 100%

49. Which of the following types of life assurance policy has a significant investment element?

    A. Level term
    B. Increasing term
    C. Family income benefit
    D. Whole-of-life

50. How can 'hedging' best be defined?

    A. Ensuring that all trades are settled on a delivery-versus-payment basis
    B. Spreading an investment portfolio across a wide range of industries and/or countries
    C. The purchase or sale of a commodity, security or other financial instrument for the purpose of offsetting the profit or loss of another security
    D. Using a central counterparty to mitigate credit risk

Answers to Multiple Choice Questions

1. D Chapter 2, Section 3

Fiscal policy involves making adjustments using government spending and taxation, while monetary policy involves making adjustments to interest rates and the money supply.

2. A Chapter 1, Section 4.2

The primary role of a custodian is the safe-keeping of assets.

3. D Chapter 2, Section 4.2

Excessive government spending can bring about an increase in inflation.

4. D Chapter 6, Section 3.3

A call option is when the buyer has the right to buy the asset at the exercise price.

5. A Chapter 3, Section 3

In a forward transaction, money does not actually change hands until some agreed future date. A buyer and seller agree on an exchange rate for any date in the future, for a fixed sum of money, and the transaction occurs on that date, regardless of what the market rates are then. The duration of the trade can be a few days, months or years.

6. A Chapter 3, Section 2.1.2

Treasury bills are normally traded in the money markets. They are usually issued weekly by or on behalf of governments and the money is used to meet the government's short-term borrowing needs.

7. C Chapter 9, Section 3.3

In a fixed rate mortgage the borrower's interest rate is set for an initial period, usually the first three or five years. If interest rates fall and perhaps stay low, the fixed rate loan can only be cancelled if a redemption penalty is paid.

8. C Chapter 4, Section 1.1

If a company closes down, often described as the company being 'wound up', the ordinary shareholders are paid after everybody else. If there is nothing left, then the ordinary shareholders get nothing.

9. D Chapter 2, Section 3.1

Central banks generally do not regulate stock markets.

10. A Chapter 5, Section 2.2

There is a possibility that the issuer will not repay the capital at maturity (ie, default risk) and the bond's value can be influenced by interest rate changes (ie, market risk).

11. D Chapter 6, Section 3

Being short means selling. An investor who is selling a call option may be forced to make a future sale to the option buyer at a price agreed today, so he or she hopes the actual price will fall.

12. D Chapter 5, Section 3.1

Treasury bills do not pay interest but instead are issued at a discount to par.

13. D Chapter 8, Section 3.2

Market abuse must satisfy at least one of three conditions and one of these conditions relates to giving a false or misleading impression of the supply, demand or value of a particular investment.

14. B Chapter 9, Section 2.2

20% divided by 2 = 10%, expressed as 0.10

1 + 0.10 = 1.10

$1.10^2 = 1.10 \times 1.10 = 1.21$

1.21 – 1 = 0.21 x 100 = 21%

15. B Chapter 9, Section 4.3

Term assurance is designed to pay out only if death occurs within a specified period.

16. C Chapter 4, Section 7

SSE Composite is the main index of China.

17. B Chapter 3, Section 2.1.2

Commercial paper is issued by companies and is effectively the corporate equivalent of a Treasury bill.

18. D Chapter 7, Section 3.3

Like other listed company shares, shares in investment trust companies are bought and sold on stock exchanges.

19. D Chapter 4, Section 6

NASDAQ operates a quote-driven trading system.

20. B Chapter 6, Section 2.2

A future is an agreement between a buyer and seller whereby the buyer agrees to pay a pre-specified amount for the delivery of a particular quantity of an asset at a future date.

21. C Chapter 5, Section 2.1

The interest is normally payable half-yearly and is based on the nominal value, ie, £1,000 x 7% x (6 ÷ 12) = £35.00.

22. C Chapter 8, Section 3.1

Only futures and options on securities are covered by the insider trading rules. Collectives are not covered by the insider trading rules.

23. C Chapter 5, Section 3.1

TIPS means Treasury Inflation-Protected Securities and therefore is a type of index-linked US government bond that will guard against the risk posed by inflation.

24. B Chapter 5, Section 7

The flat yield is calculated by taking the annual coupon and dividing by the bond's price, and then multiplying by 100 to obtain a percentage. So the calculation is (5 ÷ 112) x 100 = 4.46%.

25. D Chapter 6, Section 4.1

A swap is a type of OTC derivative.

26. C Chapter 7, Section 1.2.1

A passive fund aims to generate returns in line with a chosen index or benchmark.

27. A Chapter 3, Section 2.1.2

Commercial paper and Treasury bills are zero coupon and issued at a discount to their par value.

28. A Chapter 7, Section 2.2.1

FCPs are a type of European investment scheme similar to unit trusts, but based on a contract between the scheme manager and the investors.

29. D Chapter 4, Section 3

A mandatory corporate action with options is an action that has some sort of default option which will occur if the shareholder does not intervene, such as a rights issue.

30. A Chapter 7, Section 4

An exchange-traded fund (ETF) is an investment fund which is usually designed to track a particular index.

31. C Chapter 7, Section 6

Private equity arrangements are usually structured in different ways from retail collective investment schemes. They are usually set up as limited partnerships, with high minimum investment levels.

32. B Chapter 4, Section 3.1.6

The share price normally falls on the ex-dividend day.

33. A Chapter 4, Section 3.1.4

A capitalisation issue involves distributing bonus shares, so there is no need to subscribe any further funds.

34. B Chapter 1, Section 4.11

The International Swaps and Derivatives Association (ISDA) is the trade body for investment institutions that trade OTC derivatives.

35. D Chapter 4, Section 6

A multilateral trading facility (MTF) is an alternative method for trading equities and bonds rather than through a traditional stock exchange.

36. A Chapter 2, Section 3.1

The ECB operates to a 2% medium-term inflation target.

37. D Chapter 7, Section 2.2

The trustee is the legal owner of the assets in the trust, holding the assets for the benefit of the underlying unit holders.

38. A Chapter 3, Section 2.1.2

Settlement of money market instruments is typically achieved through the same settlement system that is used for equities and bonds, and many money market instruments, such as certificates of deposit, can be bought and sold in the same way as shares. All the other statements are true.

39. C Chapter 4, Section 3.2

Changes to a company's constitution are normally deemed to be a special resolution which requires at least 75% to vote in favour.

40. C Chapter 4, Section 4

The primary market is where new shares in a company are marketed for the first time. When these shares are subsequently resold, this is normally done on the secondary market.

41. C Chapter 5, Section 7

The yield would change from (5 ÷ 80) x 100 = 6.25% to (5 ÷ 85) x 100 = 5.88%.

42. C Chapter 6, Section 2.3

Long is the term used for the position taken by the buyer of a future.

43. C Chapter 8, Section 2.1

Layering is the second stage and involves moving the money around in order to make it difficult for the authorities to link the placed funds with the ultimate beneficiary of the money.

44. **C** **Chapter 7, Section 1.2.3**

Index trackers and actively managed funds can be combined in what is known as core satellite management.

45. **A** **Chapter 7, Section 5**

Many hedge funds can borrow funds and use derivatives to potentially enhance returns.

46. **D** **Chapter 3, Section 2.1**

100% – 20% = 80% = 0.8

2.5 ÷ 0.8 = 3.125

3.125% x $10,000 = $312.50

47. **D** **Chapter 2 , Section 4.2**

Inflation erodes the value of money and so those on fixed incomes suffer.

48. **D** **Chapter 9, Section 3.4**

Under the ijara system the bank, rather than the borrower, buys the property and, at the end of the rental period (usually 25 years), ownership is transferred to the customer.

49. **D** **Chapter 9, Section 4.2**

Whole-of-life policies are investment-based policies.

50. **C** **Chapter 7, Section 5, and Glossary**

Hedging involves buying or selling an instrument in order to hedge against the profit or loss on another security.

Syllabus Learning Map

Syllabus Unit/ Element		Chapter/ Section
Element 1	**The Financial Services Industry**	**Chapter 1**
1.1	**The Financial Services Industry** On completion, the candidate should:	
1.1.1	Know the role of the following within the financial services industry: • retail banks/commercial banks • savings institutions • investment banks • private banks • retirement schemes • insurance companies • fund managers • stockbrokers • custodians • third party administrators (TPAs) • industry trade bodies • sovereign wealth funds	5
Element 2	**The Economic Environment**	**Chapter 2**
2.1	**The Economic Environment** On completion, the candidate should:	
2.1.1	Know the factors which determine the level of economic activity: • state-controlled economies • market economies • mixed economies • open economies	2
2.1.2	Know the role of central banks	3.1
2.1.3	Know how goods and services are paid for and how credit is created	4.1
2.1.4	Understand the meaning of inflation: • measurement • impact • control	4.2, 4.3
2.1.5	Understand the impact of the following economic data: • Gross domestic product (GDP) • balance of payments • level of unemployment	4.3.2
Element 3	**Financial Assets and Markets**	**Chapter 3**
3.1	**Cash Deposits** On completion, the candidate should:	
3.1.1	Know the characteristics of fixed-term and instant access deposit accounts	2.1.1
3.1.2	Understand the distinction between gross and net interest payments	2.1.1
3.1.3	Be able to calculate the net interest due given the gross interest rate, the deposited sum, the period and tax rate	2.1.1

Syllabus Unit/ Element		Chapter/ Section
3.1.4	Know the advantages and disadvantages of investing in cash	2.1.1
3.2	**Money Market Instruments** On completion, the candidate should:	
3.2.1	Know the difference between a capital market instrument and a money market instrument	2.1.2
3.2.2	Know the definition and features of the following: • Treasury bill • commercial paper • certificate of deposit	2.1.2
3.2.3	Know the advantages and disadvantages of investing in money market instruments	2.1.2
3.3	**Property** On completion, the candidate should:	
3.3.1	Know the characteristics of property investment • commercial/residential property • direct/indirect investment	2.4
3.3.2	Know the advantages and disadvantages of investing in property	2.4
3.4	**Foreign Exchange Market** On completion, the candidate should:	
3.4.1	Know the basic structure of the foreign exchange market including: • currency quotes • settlement • spot/forward • short-term currency swaps	3

Element 4	Equities/Stocks	Chapter 4
4.1	**Equities** On completion, the candidate should:	
4.1.1	Know the features and benefits of ordinary and preference shares/ common stock and preferred stock: • dividend • capital gain • pre-emptive rights • right to vote	1
4.1.2	Be able to calculate the share dividend yield	1
4.1.3	Understand the risks associated with owning shares/stock: • price risk • liquidity risk • issuer risk • foreign exchange risk	2
4.1.4	Know the definition of a corporate action and the difference between mandatory, voluntary and mandatory with options	3
4.1.5	Know the different methods of quoting securities ratios	3.1

Syllabus Unit/ Element		Chapter/ Section
4.1.6	Understand the following terms: • bonus/scrip/capitalisation issues • rights issues/open offers • stock splits/reverse stock splits • dividend payments • takeover/merger	3.1
4.1.7	Know the purpose and format of annual company meetings	3.2
4.1.8	Know the differences between the primary market and secondary market	4
4.1.9	Understand the characteristics of depositary receipts: • American depositary receipt • global depositary receipt • dividend payments • how created/pre-release facility • rights	5
4.1.10	Know the role of stock markets	6
4.1.11	Know the types and uses of a stock exchange index	7
4.1.12	Know how shares are traded: • on-exchange/off-exchange • multilateral trading facilities • order-driven/quote-driven	6
4.1.13	Understand how settlement takes place: • process • settlement cycles	8

Element 5	Characteristics	Chapter 5
5.1	**Government Bonds** On completion, the candidate should:	
5.1.1	Understand the characteristics and terminology of bonds: • coupon • redemption • nominal value	2.1
5.1.2	Know the definition and features of government bonds: • US • UK • France • Germany • Japan	2.1 and 3
5.1.3	Know the advantages and disadvantages of investing in government bonds	2.2

Syllabus Unit/ Element		Chapter/ Section
5.2	**Corporate Bonds** On completion, the candidate should:	
5.2.1	Know the definitions and features of the following types of bond: • domestic • foreign • eurobond	6
	• asset-backed securities	5
	• zero coupon • convertible	4
5.2.2	Be able to calculate the flat yield of a bond	7
5.2.3	Know the advantages and disadvantages of investing in corporate bonds	2.2
5.2.4	Understand the role of credit rating agencies and the difference between investment and non-investment grades	2.3

Element 6	Derivatives	Chapter 6
6.1	**Derivatives Uses** On completion, the candidate should:	
6.1.1	Know the uses and application of derivatives	1.1
6.2	**Futures** On completion, the candidate should:	
6.2.1	Know the definition and function of a future	2
6.3	**Options** On completion, the candidate should:	
6.3.1	Know the definition and function of an option	3
6.3.2	Understand the following terms: • calls • puts	3
6.4	**Terminology** On completion, a candidate should:	
6.4.1	Understand the following terms: • long • short • open • close	2
	• holder • writing • premium • covered • naked	3
	• OTC • exchange-traded	1.1

Syllabus Unit/ Element		Chapter/ Section
6.5	**Derivatives/Commodity Exchanges** On completion, the candidate should:	
6.5.1	Know the function of a derivatives exchange and the products traded	5.2
6.5.2	Know the advantages and disadvantages of investing in the derivatives and commodity markets	5.3
6.6	**Swaps** On completion, the candidate should:	
6.6.1	Know the definition and function of an interest rate swap	4
6.6.2	Know the definition and function of a credit default swap	4.3

Element 7	Investment Funds	Chapter 7
7.1	**Introduction** On completion, the candidate should:	
7.1.1	Understand the benefits of collective investment	1.1
7.1.2	Know the difference between active and passive management	1.2
7.2	**Open-Ended/Mutual Funds** On completion, the candidate should:	
7.2.1	Know the characteristics and different types of open-ended fund/ mutual fund: • US • Europe	2
7.3	**Closed-Ended Investment Companies** On completion, the candidate should:	
7.3.1	Know the characteristics of closed-ended investment companies: • share classes	3
7.3.2	Understand the factors that affect the price of closed-ended investment companies	3
7.3.3	Know the meaning of the discounts and premiums in relation to closed-ended investment companies	3
7.3.4	Know how closed-ended investment companies' shares are traded	3
7.4	**Real Estate Investment Trusts (REITs)** On completion, the candidate should:	
7.4.1	Know the basic characteristics of REITs: • tax implications • property diversification • liquidity • risk	3.4
7.5	**Exchange-Traded Funds** On completion, the candidate should:	
7.5.1	Know the main characteristics of exchange-traded funds: • trading • replication methods	4

Syllabus Unit/ Element		Chapter/ Section
7.6	**Hedge Funds** On completion, the candidate should:	
7.6.1	Know the basic characteristics of hedge funds: • risks • cost and liquidity • investment strategies	5
7.7	**Private Equity** On completion, the candidate should:	
7.7.1	Know the basic characteristics of private equity: • raising finance • realising capital gain	6

Element 8	Regulation and Ethics	Chapter 8
8.1	**Introduction** On completion, the candidate should:	
8.1.1	Understand the need for regulation	1.1
8.1.2	Understand the main aims and activities of financial services regulators	1.2
8.1.3	Know the CISI Code of Conduct	4.5.2
8.1.4	Understand the key principles of professional integrity and ethical behaviour in financial services	4
8.2	**Financial Crime** On completion, the candidate should:	
8.2.1	Understand the terms that describe the three main stages of money laundering	2.1
8.2.2	Know the action to be taken by those employed in financial services if money laundering activity is suspected	2.2
8.3	**Insider Trading and Market Abuse** On completion, the candidate should:	
8.3.1	Know the offences that constitute insider trading and the instruments covered	3.1
8.3.2	Know the offences that constitute market abuse and the instruments covered	3.2

Element 9	Other Financial Products	Chapter 9
9.1	**Retirement Planning** On completion, the candidate should:	
9.1.1	Know the reasons for retirement planning	1
9.1.2	Know the basic features and risk characteristics of retirement funds: • state schemes • corporate retirement plans (defined benefit, defined contribution) • personal schemes	1
9.2	**Loans** On completion, the candidate should:	
9.2.1	Know the differences between bank loans, overdrafts and credit card borrowing	2

Syllabus Unit/ Element		Chapter/ Section
9.2.2	Know the difference between the quoted interest rate on borrowing and the effective annual percentage rate of borrowing	2
9.2.3	Be able to calculate the effective annual percentage rate of borrowing, given the quoted interest rate and frequency of payment	2
9.2.4	Know the difference between secured and unsecured borrowing	2
9.3	**Mortgages** On completion, the candidate should:	
9.3.1	Understand the characteristics of the mortgage market: • interest rates • repayment	3
9.3.2	Know the prohibition on interest under Islamic finance and the types of mortgage contracts	3.4
9.4	**Life Assurance** On completion, the candidate should:	
9.4.1	Understand the basic principles of life assurance	4
9.4.2	Know the main types of life policy: • term assurance • whole-of-life	4

Examination Specification

Each examination paper is constructed from a specification that determines the weightings that will be given to each element. The specification is given below.

It is important to note that the numbers quoted may vary slightly from examination to examination as there is some flexibility to ensure that each examination has a consistent level of difficulty. However, the number of questions tested in each element should not change by more than plus or minus 2.

Element Number	Element	Questions
1	The Financial Services Industry	2
2	Economic Environment	3
3	Financial Assets and Markets	7
4	Equities/Stocks	9
5	Bonds	5
6	Derivatives	6
7	Investment Funds	7
8	Regulation and Ethics	5
9	Other Financial Products	6
Total		**50**

CISI Associate (ACSI) Membership can work for you...

Studying for a CISI qualification is hard work and we're sure you're putting in plenty of hours, but don't lose sight of your goal!

This is just the first step in your career; there is much more to achieve!

The securities and investments industry attracts ambitious and driven individuals. You're probably one yourself and that's great, but on the other hand you're almost certainly surrounded by lots of other people with similar ambitions.

So how can you stay one step ahead during these uncertain times?

Entry Criteria:
Pass in either:

- Investment Operations Certificate (IOC), IFQ, ICWIM, Capital Markets in, eg, Securities, Derivatives, Advanced Certificates; or
- one CISI Diploma/Masters in Wealth Management paper

Joining Fee: £25 or free if applying via prefilled application form **Annual Subscription (pro rata):** £125

Using your new CISI qualification* to become an Associate (ACSI) member of the Chartered Institute for Securities & Investment could well be the next important career move you make this year, and help you maintain your competence.

Join our global network of over 40,000 financial services professionals and start enjoying both the professional and personal benefits that CISI membership offers. Once you become a member you can use the prestigious ACSI designation after your name and even work towards becoming personally chartered.

* ie, Investment Operations Certificate (IOC), IFQ, ICWIM, Capital Markets

Benefits in Summary...

- Use of the CISI CPD Scheme
- Unlimited free CPD seminars, webcasts, podcasts and online training tools
- Highly recognised designatory letters
- Unlimited free attendance at CISI Professional Forums
- CISI publications including *S&I Review* and *Change – The Regulatory Update*
- 20% discount on all CISI conferences and training courses
- Invitation to CISI Annual Lecture
- Select Benefits – our exclusive personal benefits portfolio

The ACSI designation will provide you with access to a range of member benefits, including Professional Refresher where there are currently over 60 modules available on subjects including Behavioural Finance, Cybercrime and Conduct Risk. CISI TV is also available to members, allowing you to catch up on the latest CISI events, whilst earning valuable CPD hours.

Plus many other networking opportunities which could be invaluable for your career.

Revision Express Interactive

You've bought the workbook... now test your knowledge before your exam.

Revision Express Interactive is an engaging online study tool to be used in conjunction with CISI workbooks. It contains exercises and revision questions.

Key Features of Revision Express Interactive:

- Examination-focused – the content of Revision Express Interactive covers the key points of the syllabus
- Questions throughout to reaffirm understanding of the subject
- Special end-of-module practice exam to reflect as closely as possible the standard you will experience in your exam (please note, however, they are not the CISI exam questions themselves)
- Interactive exercises throughout
- Extensive glossary of terms
- Useful associated website links
- Allows you to study whenever you like

IMPORTANT: The questions contained in Revision Express Interactive elearning products are designed as aids to revision, and should not be seen in any way as mock exams.

Price per elearning module: £35
Price when purchased with the CISI workbook: £100 (normal price: £110)

To purchase Revision Express Interactive:

call our Customer Support Centre on:
+44 20 7645 0777

or visit CISI Online Bookshop at:
cisi.org/bookshop

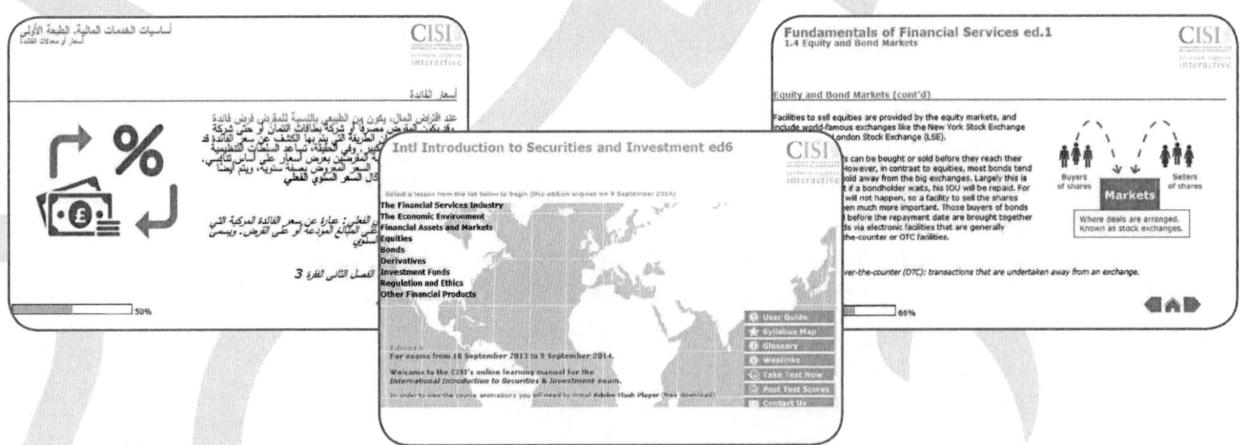

For more information on our elearning products, contact our Customer Support Centre on +44 20 7645 0777, or visit our website at cisi.org/study

Feedback to the CISI

Have you found this workbook to be a valuable aid to your studies? We would like your views, so please email us at learningresources@cisi.org with any thoughts, ideas or comments.

Accredited Training Providers

Support for examination students studying for the Chartered Institute for Securities & Investment (CISI) Qualifications is provided by several Accredited Training Providers (ATPs), including Fitch Learning and BPP. The CISI's ATPs offer a range of face-to-face training courses, distance learning programmes, their own learning resources and study packs which have been accredited by the CISI. The CISI works in close collaboration with its ATPs to ensure they are kept informed of changes to CISI examinations so they can build them into their own courses and study packs.

CISI Workbook Specialists Wanted

Workbook Authors

Experienced freelance authors with finance experience, and who have published work in their area of specialism, are sought. Responsibilities include:

- Updating workbooks in line with new syllabuses and any industry developments
- Ensuring that the syllabus is fully covered

Workbook Reviewers

Individuals with a high-level knowledge of the subject area are sought. Responsibilities include:

- Highlighting any inconsistencies against the syllabus
- Assessing the author's interpretation of the workbook

Workbook Technical Reviewers

Technical reviewers provide a detailed review of the workbook and bring the review comments to the panel. Responsibilities include:

- Cross-checking the workbook against the syllabus
- Ensuring sufficient coverage of each learning objective

Workbook Proofreaders

Proofreaders are needed to proof workbooks both grammatically and also in terms of the format and layout. Responsibilities include:

- Checking for spelling and grammar mistakes
- Checking for formatting inconsistencies

If you are interested in becoming a CISI external specialist call:

+44 20 7645 0609

or email:

externalspecialists@cisi.org

For bookings, orders, membership and general enquiries please contact our Customer Support Centre on +44 20 7645 0777, or visit our website at cisi.org